D1605993

OPENING WEDNESDAY AT A THEATER OR DRIVE-IN NEAR YOU

OPENING WEDNESDAY AT A THEATER OR DRIVE-IN NEAR YOU

THE SHADOW CINEMA OF THE AMERICAN '70s

CHARLES TAYLOR

BLOOMSBURY

NEW YORK · LONDON · OXFORD · NEW DELHI · SYDNEY

Bloomsbury USA
An imprint of Bloomsbury Publishing Plc

1385 Broadway   50 Bedford Square
New York   London
NY 10018   WC1B 3DP
USA   UK

www.bloomsbury.com

BLOOMSBURY and the Diana logo are trademarks of Bloomsbury Publishing Plc

First published 2017

Versions of these essays previously appeared in different form in the following publications:
"The Goosing of the President: *Winter Kills*" in *The Yale Review*
"Bebop/Silence: *Hickey & Boggs*" in *Los Angeles Review of Books*
"On the Hoof, On the Barrel: *Prime Cut*" in *Los Angeles Review of Books*

ISBN: HB: 978-1-63286-818-3
ePub: 978-1-63286-817-6

LIBRARY OF CONGRESS CATALOGING-IN-PUBLICATION DATA

Names: Taylor, Charles, 1961– author.
Title: Opening Wednesday at a theater or drive-in near you: the shadow
cinema of the American '70s / by Charles Taylor.
Description: New York: Bloomsbury USA, 2017.
Identifiers: LCCN 2016040877 | ISBN 9781632868183 (hardback)
Subjects: LCSH: B films—United States—History and criticism. | Motion
pictures—United State—History—20th century. | BISAC: PERFORMING ARTS /
Film & Video / History & Criticism.
Classification: LCC PN1995.9.B2 T39 2017 | DDC 791.43097309/047—dc23 LC record
available at https://lccn.loc.gov/2016040877.

2 4 6 8 10 9 7 5 3 1

Typeset by RefineCatch Limited, Bungay, Suffolk
Printed and bound in the U.S.A. by Berryville Graphics Inc., Berryville, Virginia

To my two best and most constant movie dates,
Stephanie and Dad.
And to the memory of my mom.

I'm eternally grateful that Dad didn't concern himself with which movies were age appropriate for a seven-year-old. The only criterion was that they were good, and back then, they were.

—A. J. ALBANY, *LOW DOWN*

TABLE OF CONTENTS

PREVUES OF COMING ATTRACTIONS

FORTY YEARS ON, the 1970s remain the third—and, to date, last—great period in American movies. The late teens and '20s gave us the lyrical flowering of silent movies. The '30s through the '50s, the sustained and breathless articulation of the language of classical American narrative cinema. These were the decades in which every now-familiar genre found its definitive form: Westerns, gangster films, screwball comedies and romantic comedies, musicals, war pictures, melodrama, film noir.

By the '60s those genres seemed calcified, remnants of a familiar past that prevented the now-faltering studios from acknowledging the rapidly changing present. The censorious Production Code was toppling, and the studios knew they had to win the younger, hipper audiences who wouldn't settle for the old formulas. Suddenly there was space for filmmakers who had grown up on American movies to bring a new realism to the genres they loved. Upstarts like Francis Ford Coppola, Martin Scorsese, Sam Peckinpah, Hal Ashby, Arthur Penn, Paul Mazursky, Alan J. Pakula, Brian De Palma, and Robert Altman were free to use the classic forms for work that reflected new realities, free of the official optimism to which Hollywood directors either had to accede or subvert.

There were variations on the Western (*The Wild Bunch, McCabe and Mrs. Miller*), the private-eye picture (*The Long Goodbye, The Late Show*), the gangster film (*The Godfather, Thieves Like Us*), the marital comedy (*Bob & Carol & Ted & Alice*), the musical (*Cabaret*), the women's melodrama (*Alice Doesn't Live Here Anymore*), the small-town soap opera (*The Last Picture Show*), the sex rondelet (*Shampoo*), the military comedy (*M*A*S*H*, *The Last Detail*). The new movies didn't offer audiences happy endings or other assurances. Michael Corleone doesn't get his comeuppance at the end of *The Godfather*, as the gangsters in *Scarface* and *Little Caesar* and *The Public Enemy* did. At the movie's finish, Michael has achieved a corporate ruthlessness far colder than the old-world courtliness of his crime boss father (Marlon Brando). What satisfied the audiences for *The Godfather* and the other downbeat hits of the day wasn't the old morality that Hollywood bosses—if not filmmakers—had insisted on but the exhilaration of feeling that someone had cut through the bullshit and shown something of life as they knew it to be lived.

This book is not about those landmark movies, which have been written about eloquently by critics lucky enough to be working at the time. Their work will continue to provide material for new generations of critics to offer up new insights about those works.

The focus here is on some of the movies that slipped into the background while those pictures dominated the foreground.

The title of the book, *Opening Wednesday at a Theater or Drive-in Near You*, refers to the release pattern used for horror movies, biker pictures, nudie teasers, women's prison pictures, moonshiner sagas, phony documentaries like *In Search of Noah's Ark*, Eurosleaze exploitation pictures like *Mark of the Devil* ("Rated V for Violence" and including a vomit bag with every ticket sold). These pictures were preceded a week or two in advance by saturation advertising campaigns that seemed to appear out of nowhere, deluging newspaper, radio, and TV with ads that breathlessly announced the film would be "opening Wednesday at a theater or drive-in near you!" The aim, as with a traveling carnival and side-show, was to get asses in the seats and then get the hell out of Dodge. Unlike the prestige studio movies, which were given plat-form releases, opening on a few select big-city screens and gradually making their way to more theaters and other cities—a release schedule that could keep a popular film in release for close to a year—many of the movies written about here began their commer-cial life in the second-run neighborhood houses and drive-ins—the very places where the big releases ended their theatrical lives.

Not every movie in this book opened that way. I am not dealing here with the lowest of the exploitation low. Nor (with the exception of Sam Peckinpah's *Bring Me the Head of Alfredo Garcia*) am I arguing that they constitute a series of overlooked master-pieces. It wasn't critical ignorance that kept these movies from serious consideration. When movies as extraordinary as *The Godfather* or *The Wild Bunch* or *Taxi Driver* or *Cabaret* or *The Long Goodbye* were opening every week, when critics found themselves in the enviable position of having great work to acclaim—or argue over—week in and week out, you can't exactly blame them for not paying attention to the pictures that seemed content to stay within the genre boundaries the celebrated works were exploding. Given the choice between devoting your column inches to new work from Altman, Scorsese, Coppola, Peckinpah, or Mazursky, or to a car-chase movie, to the instantly recognizable conventions of the new blaxploitation genre, to some new action movie, who could blame critics for sticking to the A list?

Most of the movies in this book did what they set out to do: make money fast. Some are good, solid pieces of moviemaking, and some are shrewdly put-together junk. Outsized claims for their greatness would only falsify their grungy, visceral appeal. But I believe these movies do share something with the A-list pictures of their time, something almost entirely missing in today's commercial American cinema. In the '70s the gritty and somewhat pessimistic nature that has always been characteristic of B movies translated into a refusal to keep bad things from happening to good characters, a resistance to handing out easy, happy endings. That's why it's possible to watch these movies now—despite the pulpiness, despite the obvious lashings of nudity and violence to satisfy the exploitation crowd—and feel as if you're being treated like an adult.

There were downsides to that lack of varnish. The critic Geoffrey O'Brien characterized the movies of the period as "rough and pitiless the way you always secretly wanted them to be," and went on:

> No major adjustments had to be made in deep plot structure.
> The grammar worked the way it always had. Merely rearrange a
> few markers, switch the goal posts. This time the good guys
> lose. The thieves get away with the money. The girl is not
> rescued but murdered. The cop didn't save anybody, he set them
> up in the first place. The babysitter wants to destroy the family.
> The government investigator was assassinated because he found
> out that the government did it.

O'Brien isn't just talking about B movies, either. If you were a constant moviegoer in the '70s you endured an extraordinary amount of hopelessness and cynicism. The U.S. was still fighting in Vietnam as the first revelations about Watergate began to surface. Watergate ended with our system of government working exactly the way it was supposed to, and a corrupt president condemned in something like the legislative equivalent of his landslide reelection. But instead of being hailed as a victory for American democracy, Watergate became a cynical confirmation of our worst suspicions: The system was rotten; all politicians were corrupt; the guilty would never pay for their crimes. When Nixon told David Frost he recognized his legacy as the cynicism young people showed about public office, he was acknowledging the psychic toll his crimes would take on Americans as his most lasting contribution to politics.

Many of the most acclaimed movies reflected the new cynicism. Even as a young moviegoer just barely in my teens, I remember going to the movies week after week and seeing that cynicism on screen. After a while the self-loathing on display led to the numbed certainty that this rotten state was just how things were and they would never get better.

I don't see that easy cynicism in the movies that are the subject of this book. Pessimism, yes, but that's a different creature. There's the sense that the deck is stacked and the characters might not amount to much. But there's a certain pleasure to be taken in the hard honesty of these pictures. There's comfort in someone leveling with you. Pessimism doesn't leave you feeling unclean the way the cheap and easy despair of some of the bigger pictures did, like *Chinatown*, which said that the corrupt power mongers would continue their figurative and literal rape of the land and the people and there was nothing to be done about it. Seeing that movie, you could forget that America had just toppled a corrupt presidency.

Forty years later the movies that are the subject of this book, many of which seemed in the '70s to be no more than disposable B pictures, are still with us, constituting something like a shadow cinema of that time. Part of that has to do with the way digital

culture, via DVD and Blu-ray and streaming, has empowered
movie cultism. Home video and digital streaming have made it
possible for fans who'd never forgotten them to once again see *The
Town That Dreaded Sundown, Jackson County Jail, The Legend of
Nigger Charley, Black Mama White Mama, Truck Stop Women,
Outlaw Blues, 'Gator Bait,* and a deluge of other pictures whose
titles suggest movies more vivid than the actual films themselves.
People who never forgot a certain Hammer horror movie, a Filipino
action movie, a bit of soft-core porn seen at just the right moment
of adolescence, a Saturday kiddie matinee of *Captain Nemo and the
Underwater City,* can engage their obsession in chat rooms and on
tribute sites, can obsess over them like, in Geoffrey O'Brien's words,
"an acolyte carrying the words of Thomas à Kempis or Bodhidharma
in his head."

For me, the staying power of these movies has to do with the
way they stand in opposition to the current juvenile state of
American movies. The infantilization of American movies that
began in 1977 with the unprecedented success of *Star Wars* has
become total. Mainstream moviemaking now caters almost exclusively to the tastes of the adolescent male fan. As they currently
stand, mainstream Hollywood releases consist almost exclusively of
superhero blockbusters, sequels, remakes, and comedies aimed at
the frat-boy sensibility, many of them excuses to squeeze out the
few extra dollars of admission charged for 3-D. Movies have
devolved back to spectacle and gimmicks, not so much movies
anymore as packages put together by studio marketing departments in the hopes of spawning or sustaining a franchise and
maybe selling a line of merchandise along the way. Reboots, the
periodic recycling of a property to lure in a new generation for
whom movies that are just four or five years old are antiques, are

factored into release schedules, which are now sketched out five years or so in advance. Theatrical runs have become temporary stops on the way to home video release, which accounts for a substantial amount of a movie's gross. Disposability is the goal, the constant determination to make the audience hungry for new product.

Consequently, what's happening in contemporary movies is not just the destruction of content but the destruction of the idea of content. What counts in most mainstream blockbusters are explosions, crashes, and constant displays of computer-generated imagery. The narratives are nonsensical, and so is the filmmaking. The incessantly moving camera and the Waring-blender editing that keeps shots to no more than two or three seconds destroy any ability to tell where characters are in physical relation to one another, thus eroding any kind of suspense and depriving us of any emotional stake in the outcome. We are not watching stories or characters anymore but brands. We're not even watching movie stars. The deluge of trailers that precede movies in theaters or the ads that adorn billboards and buses almost never mention who's in these blockbusters.

Part of this was swirling around unarticulated in my head one night a few summers back when I went to New York City's Anthology Film Archives to see Jonathan Kaplan's 1975 trucker-vigilante movie, *White Line Fever*. Anthology, founded in 1970 by, among others, underground filmmakers Jonas Mekas and Stan Brakhage, is by far the most avant-garde and daring rep house in New York, devoting its programming to experimental work as well as commercial pictures they believe deserve another look. *White Line Fever* was shown as part of a series of '70s genre movies that (at the time) were not available on home video. I went because I'd enjoyed some of Kaplan's other B movies, like the teens-on-the-rampage picture *Over the Edge*, and *Heart Like a Wheel*, a biopic about the race-car driver Shirley "Cha Cha" Muldowney. *White Line Fever* follows the standard B-movie vigilante scenario of upright hero who strikes back after being pushed too far by the corrupt bad guys. Except that the movie was filled with recognizable details of day-to-day working-class life. The struggling trucker hero Carrol Jo (Jan-Michael Vincent) and his factory-worker wife, Jerri (Kay Lenz), eat spaghetti for dinner for days on end and don't own a set of matching sheets. When Jerri has to go to court to testify for Carrol Jo, who's been indicted on a trumped-up assault charge, she wears a polyester-print shirt dress with pink collar and cuffs. It's the type of thing a woman would put on for church or to apply for a bank loan, what she'd wear when she wanted to make a good impression. It's easy to imagine Jerri treating herself to the dress, thinking how fashionable it looks compared to her usual jeans and ladies' western shirts, and never imagining she'd have to wear it to try and keep her husband out of jail.

But all this is nothing compared with a scene that takes place midway through the movie. Jerri is talking to her brother, who's also Carrol Jo's best friend. She's just found out she's pregnant. She and Carrol Jo have wanted to start a family but intended to wait until they were on their feet financially. Jerri knows that if she tells Carrol Jo she's pregnant, he'll work himself ragged to make ends meet. She doesn't want that. And so she confides in her brother that she's going to have an abortion and doesn't intend to tell her husband. She doesn't go through with it (for reasons that have more to do with the revenge-movie mechanics of the plot rather than any ideological conviction), but that's less important than the matter-of-factness of Jerri's reasoning and Kay Lenz's plainspoken reading of the lines. The scene leaves open the possibility that Jerri will regret her choice. The movie doesn't hold the realities of human behavior hostage to ideology, and we can see that Jerri would like to be able to bring this pregnancy to term. But regret isn't the same thing as shame, and there's no shame in the character. The consistent assumption is that this is a woman's choice, even if she's married, even if she's making it for economic reasons. And this in a movie whose association with trucking and with Carrol Jo's record of heroism in Vietnam—not to mention the country music on the soundtrack—tagged it as directed at a rural, probably conservative audience. Today it's a shock when an indie picture like *Obvious Child*, starring the comic Jenny Slate, manages to be unapologetic about abortion. It's unthinkable that a contemporary mainstream movie, even one upfront about its liberal politics, would portray a woman making the choice at all without falling prey to the shame and regret that never occurred to the makers of *White Line Fever*.

After seeing it, I began looking at other films from the period, some I'd not seen in years, or some that I'd missed and, because of DVD and Blu-ray, was finally able to see for the first time. Not everything provided as much of a shock. The appeal of many was precisely that they offered moviegoers a few hours free from responsibility and morality. Their grunginess offered dirty thrills, often without the distracting trappings of quality found in the big studios' prestige releases. The fun of watching Peter Fonda and Susan George as a fugitive robber and his trampy girlfriend in *Dirty Mary Crazy Larry* was seeing them tear up country roads in a '66 Chevy Impala (later a '69 Dodge Charger R/T 440), to the annoyance of a hard-ass cop on their tails (played by squinting, purse-lipped Vic Morrow, who'd have looked pissed off if he were standing in front of Jesus on Judgment Day). The fun was in the low-down, foul-mouthed atmosphere, as when an angry Fonda says to George, "You try a stunt like that again and I'll braid your tits." (I still remember the mouths of my mom and my Aunt Floss dropping open when they heard that line during the outing to see the movie that my cousin Judy and I had conned our families into.)

What I did find in the movies I chose to write about here was the connection to the world, and to real-life emotions—not to mention the craft—that today's blockbusters and remakes and churned-out franchises work so hard to avoid. The best genre movies, no matter how rooted in the conventions of Westerns, detective stories, adventure stories, or noir, have always involved adult emotions: temptation, guilt, sexual desire, the pull of responsibility. The violence in those films is wrought and suffered on a scale far more direct than the explosions and anonymous mass killings of today's big-budget action spectaculars. In the best genre films, we're immersed in a world where decisions have to be made and consequences have to be endured. No one would mistake the 1975 *Hard Times*, Walter Hill's Depression-era tale of bare-knuckle boxers, for a documentary. But when a waitress tells Charles Bronson that his nickel cup of coffee entitles him to only one refill, you get an immediate sense of the desperate straits of the time, the need to weigh every penny. The small towns, gas stations, and two-lane highways, the diners of *Vanishing Point*, *Two-Lane Blacktop*, *Citizens Band*, and other movies, are all but absent from today's screens, as are the seamy views of American cities that you get in *Prime Cut*, *Hickey & Boggs*, and *Cisco Pike*.

Opening Wednesday at a Theater or Drive-in Near You does not claim to be a comprehensive history of American genre movies of the '70s. Many readers may never have heard of most of the movies in this book. That is precisely my point. I wish these essays to serve as both introduction and explication. My method is discrete, more akin to a mosaic than an overview, drawing on elements of sociology, history, and political commentary. I believe good criticism must evoke the experience of encountering a work, and that's what I aim to do here. I want not just to describe the experience of seeing these movies, not just to suggest what keeps them worth watching, but to use them to unlock their time, to suggest what they managed to contain of America in the moment they were made.

When I finished the book I realized that three American filmmakers kept turning up as touchstones again and again. I offer these brief sketches for the reader.

Preston Sturges, the greatest American comic filmmaker of the sound era, took in territory that included both high society (*The Lady Eve*, *The Palm Beach Story*) and small-town America (*The Miracle of Morgan's Creek*, *Hail the Conquering Hero*). But whether we're in a New York supper club or the local diner, democracy in a Sturges film is a kind of shared delirium, a meeting place of the odd, the obsessed, the agitated, the pixilated, the softheaded, and the wisecrackers. The films are suffused with a cracked warmth, Sturges's realization that there is nothing so odd as the ordinary American.

Howard Hawks, a conservative in real life, was classical Hollywood's great modernist. In Hawks's films such as *Only Angels Have Wings*, *To Have and Have Not*, *The Thing from Another World*, *Rio Bravo*, *Hatari!*, and *El Dorado*, communities are always makeshift groups of drifters who coalesce around some common task or purpose. They may be trying to escape a past in which what they are has been held against them, but none try to escape their identities. The characters meet the task at hand by not thinking much beyond the present. Hawks's groups constitute outposts where democracy works as it was meant to, where the group becomes the place in which every member finds the highest and best version of their own individualism. The communion of the films comes from the fierce respect for personal competence, an honest (but never cruel) acknowledgment of flaws, and a belief that human beings have the strength to transcend those flaws.

If Hawks was Hollywood's great modernist, John Ford was its great traditionalist, and I confess he is a director who has often won my respect more than my love. But I would love John Ford if he had done nothing more than *Stagecoach,* a film that occupies the place in American movies that *The Adventures of Huckleberry Finn* does in American literature. The film is often called the greatest traditional Western and yet nothing in it is settled. In *Stagecoach,* Ford explores the essential tension of American life, the desire to belong and the desire to light out for the territories. And it's a film where the most honorable community consists of outsiders—an outlaw, a prostitute, a drunk, a gambler—who come together to save each other after being rejected by the pillars of frontier civilization, the people who've already transformed the pioneer spirit into a nascent version of small-town prudishness. At the end of *Stagecoach,* the outlaw and the prostitute ride off together to make a home while the drunk and the sheriff wave them good-bye, praying they will be spared "the blessings of civilization."

Sturges's oddballs, Hawks's adventurers, and Ford's outcasts carry with them a faint hint of the disreputability that colors each of the films in this book. More important, these are the three film-makers who, for me, have been most involved with exploring the tension between community and individuality, between responsibility and the pursuit of happiness that are at the heart of American life and American art. That none of them would have described their work in such a way is part of its greatness.

Nor am I interested in reducing the movies in this book to easily digestible themes. Instead, I want to suggest that the reach of an extraordinary moment in American filmmaking extended to films that were overlooked and made on the cheap. The thrill of going to see the big mainstream American movies of the '70s was that of being present at a time when remarkable filmmakers extended the traditions of our movie past to reflect the attitudes and concerns of our present. It was an all-too-brief period when artists ruled.

Now, when it's the studio marketing departments who rule, and commercial movies are made by directors who barely qualify as craftsmen, let alone artists, these pictures—which presented themselves so modestly and which seemed disposable to so many—showcase a level of craft and candor absent from the current movies pitched to us week after week as events. The new blockbusters, often taking advantage of 3-D or IMAX screens, seem to shrink while we're watching them. The movies in *Opening Wednesday*, without a shred of ostentation, presented a vision that couldn't be contained by the confines of a drive-in screen. For years moviegoers had been watching the characters on the big screen walk off into the sunset or into the moodiness of a nighttime city fog. Sitting in their cars at the drive-in, or in their seats at the tattered and second-run movie palaces that played these Westerns and action movies and crime thrillers and rock 'n' roll pictures, audiences could feel they were able to enter into something just as big: a vision of a troubled and tattered but still-vast America.

ON THE HOOF, ON THE BARREL: *PRIME CUT*

*And so tonight—to you, the great silent majority of my fellow
Americans—I ask for your support . . .*

*The more support I can have from the American people, the sooner
that pledge can be redeemed; for the more divided we are at home, the
less likely the enemy is to negotiate at Paris.*

Let us be united for peace. Let us also be united against defeat.

*Because let us understand: North Vietnam cannot defeat or humiliate the
United States. Only Americans can do that.*

—PRESIDENT RICHARD NIXON, NOVEMBER 3, 1969

"EVERYBODY WANTS WHAT I got. Grade A. Raised special. Course, we
gotta keep 'em a little doped up. All the livestock gets their shots."
That's Gene Hackman as the meat magnate named Mary Ann (yes,
Mary Ann—the moniker may be a jesting nod to John Wayne, né
Marion Morrison) in Michael Ritchie's 1972 *Prime Cut*. The livestock he's talking about are the girls he keeps doped up to sell as sex
slaves, girls who've been raised in the orphanage he bankrolls for
the purpose, tended to just like the steers at his Kansas City stock-
yards. "Cow flesh, girl flesh," he says, "'s all the same to me." Mary
Ann, whose packing plant is also a cover for his business selling
dope and girls, owes five hundred g's to the Chicago mob. The last
guy sent to collect went back to Chi-town as a string of hot dogs.
The new collection agent, Lee Marvin's Nick, doesn't play that shit.

"Nobody liked the hot dogs," he tells Mary Ann. Mary Ann is a nightmare version of the tin-horn power brokers who lurk on the edges of Preston Sturges's small-town comedies. The first time we see Mary Ann, he's sitting in the center of a long table, flanked by his cronies, chowing down on a heaping helping of innards. "You eat guts," says Nick. "Yeah," says Mary Ann, "I *like* 'em." He's a Midwestern Saturn devouring his son, the emblem of a country that was devouring all its sons.

Released in June 1972, nearly three years after Nixon's silent-majority speech and with America still mired in Vietnam, *Prime Cut* was reviewed largely as if it were a piece of rotting meat left out for audiences to smell. "It is as unsavory and unappetizing as a cheaper grade of packaged meat that is beginning to spoil," sniffed the *Boston Globe*. In the *New York Times*, Vincent Canby, deciding the movie was beneath him, called it "sick making and essentially silly."

The disgust focused on the credit sequence. We're touring Mary Ann's meatpacking plant, following the journey of the cows from being herded in to being wrapped in cellophane. A minute or so into the sequence we catch a glimpse of a man's bare buttocks in the midst of cows headed to the slaughter. Then, watching trimmed meat shanks progressing along a conveyor belt, we notice one of them is wearing a watch. The capper is a man's dress shoe amid the discarded bits. It's a neat, economical depiction of flesh reduced to packaged product, all set to a lulling bit of Muzak from composer Lalo Schifrin (a mockery of the kind of music that used to be piped into factories to placate workers). Vincent Canby assured his readers this was all done in "frightfully good taste." What Canby, all insular urbanity, missed is that the frightfully good taste is used to point out the worst taste of all. Ritchie doesn't go in for shots of cattle suffering or being killed. By filming a sequence in a slaughterhouse where no blood is visible, by reducing mass slaughter to assembly-line proficiency, Ritchie suggests the wicked juxtaposition that was loose in American life: the manner in which the continuing deaths of American soldiers in Vietnam was being sold to the public in such morally untroubled terms. *Prime Cut* is a brutalist satire of the America the silent majority was trying to hold on to masquerading as a mob-enforcer tale.

For that silent majority to whom Nixon appealed on that night in 1969, the real America was a bulwark against hippies, antiwar demonstrators, black people who no longer knew their place. Cities were jungles populated by psycho killers, muggers, junkies, just as they were portrayed in *Dirty Harry* and *Death Wish*. Any decent American who had to pass through them for one reason or another was entering the home-front war zone. "Chicago!" Mary Ann says when he learns that's where Nick is working these days, his false, bright tone playing at being the country mouse who sure is impressed to know someone working in the big city.

But the contempt is palpable. For the silent majority, Chicago was the place where, in '68, those hippie draft dodgers ran amuck—until the cops pounded some fear into them. That a government commission then blamed *the police* for rioting was, for Nixon's silent majority, a measure of just how unhinged America had become. Mary Ann speaks for all those Americans when he says, "Chicago's crumbling; there's nothing left there anymore but kids and old men. What hasn't been burned down has been shot out, picked over . . . Who's runnin' it? Black boys, Puerto Ricans. They got their own way of doing things. You talk their spic talk? Whadda they got anybody wants? Rats and garbage. You know what Chicago is? Chicago's a sick old sow grunting for fresh cream. What it deserves is slop. Someday they're gonna boil that town down for fat. Here it's different. This is the heartland."

Prime Cut is a sardonic report from the battle being waged to define what America was and who it was for. It sums up not just the American separatism that had already reared its head—Nixon's southern strategy; the murders of protesting students at Kent State and Jackson State; hard hats beating up protesters in lower Manhattan four days after Kent State while stockbrokers cheered them on—but anticipates the yahoo rhetoric that was to come—Reagan reviving the segregationist creed of "states' rights"; Sarah Palin talking about "the real America." This is the history that's both behind and in front of Mary Ann's speech, and it's as explicitly political as Robert Dillon's script gets. It's enough. Dillon puts the rhetoric of American separatism, of what amounts to a disbelief in democracy itself, right where it belongs—in the mouth of a thug.

Most of the time, *Prime Cut* operates in an oblique, foxy manner. On one level *Prime Cut* is a fish-out-of-water story with Marvin's Nick as the fish. The joke is that a big-city mob enforcer is in much more danger in the Kansas City heartland than any Kansan would be in Chicago. The movie's view of the sticks goes right back to *Nothing Sacred* in 1937 when New York reporter Fredric March sets foot in a small Vermont town and is greeted by a little kid who, for no reason at all, runs out of his front yard and sinks his teeth into March's leg. Part of that movie heritage is also Diana Lynn as the alarmingly practical kid sister in *The Miracle of Morgan's Creek*. Summing up the poor schnook her pregnant older sister is strong-arming into making an honest woman of her, Lynn says, "He was made for it, like the turkey for the ax."

It's easy to imagine Michael Ritchie having a soft spot for the likes of Diana Lynn. He had no use for false innocence. The Little

League team in his 1976 comedy *The Bad News Bears* are grumpy, foulmouthed, and supremely sore losers.

Ritchie, a native of Waukesha, Wisconsin, was just as amused by small towners and odd ducks as Preston Sturges and as Jonathan Demme was in *Citizens Band, Melvin and Howard, Something Wild,* and *Married to the Mob,* just not as benevolent as either of them. Ritchie doesn't condescend to the drunken coaches and used-car salesman and corrupt small-town pols and stage mothers in *The Bad News Bears* and *Smile* (a satire of teen beauty pageants) and the HBO movie *The Positively True Adventures of the Alleged Texas Cheerleader-Murdering Mom* (it was about exactly what the title said). But he wants the audience to take delight in his hard-heartedness. Ritchie, like Sturges and Demme, knew that boosterism and patriotism were often the first refuges of scoundrels. But Ritchie, working when Vietnam was winding down and Watergate was gearing up, couldn't be as sanguine, or as forgiving.

Appealing to the silent majority, and a few months later announcing the expansion of the war into Cambodia and Laos, Nixon could talk about all the deaths that were to come in terms of "winning the peace." By then Americans could see the reality of the war in *Life* magazine's weekly atrocity photo spread and in the footage on any nightly network news broadcast. *Prime Cut* brings home the mechanized slaughter of the war as packaged hot dogs.

Prime Cut isn't steeped in the self-loathing that marred some other American movies of the era. Outrage wasn't Ritchie's bag. This sly little genre picture takes its cue from Lee Marvin's decision to play a mob soldier as deadpan put-on artist.

At one point Nick bums a lift from a teenager cruising in a pickup and thanks him by pressing a few dollars on him, saying "Thanks for the lift, kid. Buy your club a case of beer." Marvin lets you hear exactly what's beneath that flip benevolence: the disbelief of a sharpster who finds himself in Squaresville.

Marvin is smack in the movie tradition of the hard-nosed American. Jeering at the cornball side of ordinary American life wasn't an invention of the counterculture. The city types who populated screwball comedies often found themselves at odds with the rubes they ran into. Claudette Colbert and Clark Gable go into a hayseed routine to hide from detectives in *It Happened One Night*; polltaker Fred MacMurray finds himself in the midst of a clan of killer hillbillies in the delirious *Murder, He Says*. But in 1972, when many Americans were clinging to tradition and familiarity to prop up failing support for a losing war—or just to condemn the funny new ideas that had gotten into people's heads—making fun of the Mayberry crowd carried a sting that was sharper than just a city slicker making fun of the hicks. In *Prime Cut*, Ritchie complicates things by being unable to either believe in that tradition or to dismiss it.

The movie is chock-full of American iconography. There are country fairs where ribbons are awarded to livestock and baked goods and fresh milk, farms worked by strapping blue-eyed blonds in overalls, amber waves of grain, white clapboard houses in the beautiful countryside. And every one of these bits of Americana is intruded on by violence or bloodlust or leering fantasy. The farm boys are the hired muscle protecting a dope and sexual-slavery business. The amber waves of grain are populated by killers or by wheat threshers trying to mow down a runaway girl and her protector. That picture-perfect white house is a brothel in training for girls who'll be shot full of dope and sold to the highest bidder. In this movie, it's not just America's sons being devoured, but its daughters, too.

Mary Ann's auction—which takes place in an open-air barn featuring hay-filled pens of naked girls, all of them doped to the gills; the customers, middle-aged men in their Sears sports coats, filling themselves with free barbecue and booze, mill around ogling the merchandise—is slave market as livestock exhibition. The scene epitomizes why this movie with almost no blood and only occasional fights or gunplay feels so bruising, why critics were so disgusted by it. Ritchie is working in that dangerous place where a viewer can either be repulsed or see the grim, mordant humor. His satire teeters on the edge of being heavy-handed. What keeps it from falling over? Perhaps that Ritchie's satire is more wicked than vitriolic, and perhaps that he refuses to give in to contempt.

The '70s gave us plenty of movies that didn't bother to disguise their contempt for America. Characters were piggy racists or warmongers; the settings, whether country club or small town, oozed corruption and rot and garishness. Ritchie and his cinematographer Gene Polito don't divorce themselves from their surroundings, don't ignore what their eyes are telling them. This gangster picture takes place mostly in daylight. Polito, composing in a wide Panavision frame, bathes the movie in clean, bright sunlight. The country-fair sequence (Mary Ann has arranged to meet Nick there to settle their business) begins with a facile satirical touch: a high school marching band playing an off-key version of "America the Beautiful." Ritchie doesn't stick with that easy smart-assed approach. For a couple of minutes the director allows Polito's camera to simply roam the fair, taking in the sights and the people. What we see might constitute a short list of clichéd Americana: a marching band; cows and pigs being groomed for judging; hawkers selling souvenirs; the sound of a carousel; a hog-tying competition; stacks of preserves for sale; a pie-eating contest; kids pitching rings around bottle necks or tossing baseballs to win a stuffed animal or just laughing happily on rides. It looks like a pleasant way to spend an afternoon, and it isn't presented as a lie. Essentially, it's a documentary sequence. The people we see are real, some of the faces are young, some are grizzled, and they've been filmed having a day out at a real fair, which may be why nothing looks hackneyed.

This isn't a rotten or corrupt America, and it isn't a clichéd one. It's an America that, in the midst of Vietnam and the Nixon years, still exists—and not as a relic. This way of life doesn't look as if it's going anywhere soon. And yet, without anything like mournfulness or regret but also without condescension, Ritchie is showing it to us from the point of view of someone who can't join in. It's a far gentler rejection than Mary Ann's rejection of the city, but it's still a rejection.

Of course, the hominess of a country fair doesn't tell the whole story. The heartland was also the place where parents were getting notices that their sons had been killed in Vietnam. In C. D. B. Bryan's heartrending piece of home-front reportage, 1976's *Friendly Fire*, that news comes to Peg and Gene Mullen of La Porte City, Iowa. Bryan recounts how these two family farmers became antiwar activists when their own son Michael was killed—as it turns out, by American fire. The scene when neighbors come over to commiserate with Peg and Gene, the women gathering in one room, the men in another, turns into a wake, not just for Michael but for an America these people had always assumed would be there.

The men are doing what their generation of men had always done: offering stoic camaraderie for one of their own in a time of tragedy. And yet Bryan describes how, man by man, they break down in tears of confused frustration. Nothing in their lives, the patriotism they had been brought up with, the understanding that sometimes young men were called on to sacrifice their lives for their country, had prepared them for this. They can't reconcile those beliefs with a war that, they have finally to admit, they don't understand.

That unwanted knowledge is implicit in the fairground sequence. Ritchie doesn't go in for easy contempt towards the heartlanders in front of his camera, but he senses that the life they are living cannot encompass the questions that are being imposed on it. That ambivalence is why it's fitting that we see so much of the movie through Nick's eyes.

Was there ever a movie tough guy as contained as Lee Marvin? Long and slim, though with a cruel, meaty mouth, Marvin submerged all the threat within himself. You could see that in the way he chose implied menace over bluster, in the way he hid the snarl of his voice inside a purr. In Marvin's early film appearances he could be frighteningly psycho, most famously as Marlon Brando's motorcycle-gang rival in *The Wild One* and as the hood in *The Big Heat* (1953) who throws a pot of boiling coffee in Gloria Grahame's face. But just two years later, in *Bad Day at Black Rock*, Marvin, playing a desert-town thug out to intimidate a mysterious newcomer played by Spencer Tracy, left the hulking bad-guy theatrics to Ernest Borgnine. Marvin conveyed a threat simply by stretching out his lanky, uninvited frame on Tracy's hotel-room bed. By the time he teamed with Clu Gulager as half of a pair of hit men in Don Siegel's 1964 film *The Killers*, Marvin was giving us the hood as put-on artist. Marvin and Gulager are the forerunners of the hit men–lovers Gig Young and Robert Webber would play ten years later in *Bring Me the Head of Alfredo Garcia*. They radiate a serene contempt for every bit of normalcy and kindness they encounter, in a way that makes the musclemen of so many past gangster movies look like guys who huffed and puffed up the stairs when they could have taken the elevator. The sardonicism of Marvin's performance foreshadows the career that was to follow. By the time of John Boorman's splintered and bitter revenge saga *Point Blank* (1967), Marvin had become an almost subterranean actor. The threat of violence was there but not the overt warning signs. Action heroes could be cold (Clint Eastwood) or stoic (Charles Bronson) or cool (Steve McQueen). Marvin was something else, an action star who refined threat into something approaching elegance. In *Prime Cut* he acts as if he's privy to a joke no one else is in on. That's what makes him a perfect choice for a movie that submerges its satire in action-movie mechanics. It may also have been what guaranteed that the audiences in tune with the movie's satirical vision would stay away, while the ones targeted by it might be drawn in.

By the time the new Hollywood of Peckinpah and Coppola and Dennis Hopper and Bob Rafelson and others started to arrive in the late '60s and early '70s, action movies, genre movies in general, were drawing a mainstream audience who were aesthetically, and maybe politically, conservative. A cop movie or a gangster picture or a heist picture was not going to chop up the time frame, or leave the plot shrouded in ambiguity, or dwell on its own ambivalence or alienation (which is why it would be years before the dazzling *Point Blank* was recognized as one of the key films of its era). Audiences put off by the new way of making movies could go to a genre picture knowing what they were going to get. And by 1972 Marvin had become a staple of action movies—some of them, like *The Dirty Dozen* (1967), were big hits. Young, hip audiences wanted the new style of moviemaking. They weren't Marvin's audience. The audiences who did go to Lee Marvin movies, just as the ones who stayed away, knew it would hold no arty surprises.

The poster for *Prime Cut* promised business as usual. It featured a picture of Marvin, his face contorted in rage, brandishing a machine gun and, next to it, a picture of Hackman wielding a meat cleaver. The tagline: "Lee Marvin & Gene Hackman. Together They're Murder," a routine slogan to describe a routine tough-guy outing. The only link the movie had to the youth market is Poppy, the girl Nick rescues from Mary Ann's flesh market, played, in her first speaking part, by Sissy Spacek.

It's an odd role. Poppy isn't a hippie, as almost every young female character on drugs or in the sex trade was in '70s movies. Poppy isn't involved in either by choice. Whether that registered with audiences is another matter. As the counterculture imploded, teen runaways and drug casualties were tabloid fodder, always to be found in cautionary episodes of TV series like *The Mod Squad* and *Dragnet*. To large portions of America, teenagers in trouble had no one but themselves to blame. Avoiding clichés in this as in everything else, *Prime Cut* doesn't point fingers, nor does it hold up "the kids" as the salvation for uptight, hypocritical America.

Instead, Ritchie and Dillon understand that the moralistic tales about wayward girls have always provided as much titillation as tsk-tsk. It was a short hop from *Lolita* to the comic-pornographic fantasies of Terry Southern and Mason Hoffenberg's *Candy* (*Candide* retold as the story of a sexy American teen) to the free-love-practicing hippie girls who became a staple of middle-class male sexual fantasies. "American men . . . dwelt obsessively on a single image of despoiled innocence," wrote Geoffrey O'Brien in *Dream Time: Chapters from the Sixties*.

Playboy models started wearing body paint and headbands or flashing peace signs. Every moviegoer knew that, at some point, the groovy young nubiles who appeared on screen would be ogled by Rotary Club types. (The sight, in Russ Meyer's delirious *Beyond the Valley of the Dolls*, of one hapless straight getting into bed with a swinging cutie while wearing his black dress socks and garters finished off squares in one quick image.)

For the most part *Prime Cut* avoids the lascivious come-on. One reason is the melting beauty of the young Sissy Spacek. When Poppy wakes up in Nick's hotel suite (he's spent the night sitting up in a chair, watching over her in her sleep), her impossibly big eyes take in the standard Hilton good taste—the wood paneling and oil paintings of flowers—and she announces, "I never saw anything so pretty." Nick has bundled Poppy out of Mary Ann's auction after hearing her desperate, whispered "Help me." It's less an impulse than a code of ethics. According to Marvin's biographer, Dwayne Epstein, Marvin refused to play a scene in Dillon's script in which Nick slept with Poppy. Marvin was right. Not because he's playing Nick as a white knight. Nick is, after all, there to collect a debt for the mob. Marvin makes Nick's decision to act as Poppy's protector seem not just a matter of ethics but a matter of taste. Unlike Mary Ann, Nick doesn't eat guts.

Marvin manages to hold on to that sense of taste even, in the sequence that follows, as the movie comes close to losing its own. Nick orders Poppy clothes from the ladies' shop in the lobby. When she awakes, there's an array of gift boxes next to her. From one she takes out a long green halter-top number, so diaphanous you can see her breasts when she puts it on. This is what she wears when Marvin escorts her to dinner in the hotel dining room, and what follows is a remarkable screwed-up scene that takes aim at middle-aged men's sexual fantasies of hip young girls, and very nearly falls into those fantasies.

The hotel dining room is like an exhibit from the American Museum of Natural History, a stiff version of American formal dining that no longer exists. Even (or especially) in the context of 1972, it's airless, lifeless. There's a quartet that seems to have been there since the Hoover administration playing "Jeanie with the Light Brown Hair." A line of waiters and waitresses stand at attention, ready to cater to the largely empty room. The blue velvet chair cushions look as if they will exude cigar smoke with the merest application of pressure. The average age of the diners appears to be deceased. Poppy, of course, turns heads. Ritchie includes a shot of women clucking disapproval over her dress. There's some lovely byplay in which Nick, without saying a word or calling undue attention to Poppy's embarrassment, points out to her the correct spoon with which to eat her consommé. Just as Poppy seems to be getting over her awkwardness at being in so fancy a setting, Nick notices her looking self-consciously over his shoulder. He turns his head to see a fat middle-aged man who has turned in his chair to stare openly at her. In a moment that sums up the quiet menace Marvin was capable of, Nick simply stares at the man. Just stares. And, alarmed, the rotund voyeur turns hastily back to his meal.

The moment verges on hypocrisy. Ritchie has included a clumsy close-up of Spacek's breasts, as if we needed to be reminded what the diners are staring at. And there's no doubt the dress has been chosen to get some skin into the movie. But it's not clumsy enough to bollix the larger point of the scene. Despite the movie's momentary betrayal of Spacek, you can't shake the contrast between her freshness and the desiccated flesh surrounding her, people dried up not so much by age as by the stultifying propriety that has mummified the room and mummified them. Is this why silent-majority America is so bothered by the young, because they resent that they haven't smothered themselves in the same way?

The scene is uncomfortable both because Ritchie temporarily loses control and because you can't blame anyone for looking at the fresh, lovely, young Sissy Spacek and desiring her. But you see that man appraising her, his scumminess undisguised by his middle-class respectability, and you hear in your head Mary Ann's description of Chicago: a sick old sow grunting for fresh cream.

Prime Cut gives us an America rapacious for flesh. Cow flesh, girl flesh, it's all the same. And unmentioned, unacknowledged, not even talked about on the radio, which always seems to be broadcasting only the weather report, is the young male flesh being made fodder for Vietnam. When Nick and Poppy, chased into a wheat field by Mary Ann's gunmen, are trying to keep out of the path of an oncoming wheat thresher trying to kill them, they're on the verge of being just two more carcasses waiting to be ground up. There are eerily beautiful shots of Marvin's silver-haired head peeking tentatively above the tips of the surrounding wheat, a phantom in the midst of killing fields. At times Nick seems like the last man in America whose appetite is under control. Along with the obligatory tough-guy shot of whiskey and a sip of coffee to stay awake, the only things he consumes in the entire movie are a cup of vichyssoise and a glass of milk.

That doesn't mean he's one of those hit-men ascetics like Alain Delon in *Le Samouraï* or James Caan in *Thief*, the type who might ponder some Alan Watts as soon as make sure his weapon is in working order. Marvin's Nick is the riddle of *Prime Cut*. What does he want? Power? Money? He doesn't show any hunger for more than he has. Redemption? You could no more imagine Lee Marvin redeemed—or wanting to be—than you could imagine

Julie Andrews summoning the powers of Satan. Nick doesn't have any moral problem with his job. He just wants to do it well and with as little fuss as possible. He's disgusted by Mary Ann because he's repelled by waste and by vulgarity. But Nick hasn't dropped out like the counterculture heroes of *Vanishing Point*, *Two-Lane Blacktop*, and *Cisco Pike*. In some strange way, Nick is the only character in the movie who has ideals. And, significantly, in a time of war, one of those ideals is one that American military power has abandoned. When Nick saves that poor, naïve hippie girl, he isn't making a covert bid for saving himself. He's simply paying attention to what everyone else in the picture ignores: the collateral damage.

THE CHALLENGER: *VANISHING POINT*

Everyone who's seen *Vanishing Point* remembers the car: a gleaming white 1970 Dodge Challenger, so aerodynamically sleek it appears to have reversed the laws of nature. This car doesn't look as if it displaces the air but as if the air itself parts to make way for it.

Vanishing Point opens on a Sunday morning in a California desert town a few minutes before what will be the end of that Challenger's ride. It then circles back about thirty-six hours to late Friday night in Denver when the car first makes the acquaintance of the man who'll be its driver, Barry Newman's Kowalski. The details of Kowalski's work are kept deliberately vague. He delivers cars. For whom or why is never explained, but the job doesn't seem exactly aboveboard. Hitting Denver on a Friday a few minutes before midnight to drop off one model, Kowalski immediately announces he needs to set out on the next job. His boss tries to get him to take some time off, but within minutes Kowalski is hitting up a buddy for some speed and betting him he can make it to San Francisco by Sunday morning. The movie then works its way forward to end where it begins, that sleepy California town and Kowalski on his way to the finish line that the cops have imposed on both him and the Challenger.

How many moviegoers have obsessed over Kowalski's Challenger? Quentin Tarantino's *Death Proof* is virtually a cautionary tale about the dangers of *Vanishing Point* fandom. The sublime movie stuntwoman Zoë Bell, playing herself (or a version of herself), is so infatuated with the memory of the movie, and particularly the memory of Barry Newman driving that car, that she nearly gets herself and some friends killed playing daredevil in the Challenger she finds for sale on a rural Texas farm.

And yet, for a movie that inspired Tarantino's retro grindhouse fantasy, *Vanishing Point* isn't exactly a thrill-a-minute action extravaganza. Next to the stillness of the other significant racing movie of the era, Monte Hellman's *Two-Lane Blacktop*, it looks like *Smokey and the Bandit*. But for long swatches the Challenger is swallowed up by the landscapes that Kowalski drives through on his quest to stay in motion. We see the mountains of Utah, the deserts in Nevada and around Sonora, California. Except for a few small towns along the way that look as if they could be packed up and cleared away overnight, nothing of civilization beyond a strip of asphalt has encroached on any of it. The cinematographer, John Alonzo, is partial to vistas of these landscapes taken from considerable heights, shots held so rock-steady, we might be seeing them through God's own steady eyes. In the midst of those settings, Kowalski's speeding Challenger and the sedans of the cops who pursue him across three states are all reduced to specks.

The opening shot, a slow pan that takes in a Shell station and a diner wistfully named after Route 66, makes it seem as if we might have stumbled into a ghost town. Eventually, people turn up to see the outlaw driver being reported about on radio and TV. None of these folks look like movie extras. The director, Richard C. Sarafian, and Alonzo give them a documentary particularity. One random onlooker, a man in a cowboy hat seen in silhouette through the window of an abandoned house, the fly screen hanging from the frame, blowing aimlessly in the breeze, looks like a figure from the past who has somehow turned up in an abandoned present.

There is no community in *Vanishing Point*, just the land and the few loners who inhabit various corners of it. There's an old desert rat (the veteran actor Dean Jagger) who catches poisonous snakes and trades them for coffee and beans and flour. There's the hippie biker a flagging Kowalski meets towards the end of his ride who provides him with uppers. And there's the biker's girl, riding naked on her motorbike around their desert shack, who offers Kowalski a more intimate pick-me-up. He's flattered, turns her down in the most gentlemanly way, and makes her feel she's given him the world when she manages to find him a smoke—a straight one.

Two years before *Vanishing Point*, the bikers in *Easy Rider* had set out to find America. But America is nearly always more potent as an idea of freedom, an idea that always exists somewhere other than where the hero happens to be, than as a physical place. The characters with whom Kowalski shares some fleeting bond—that desert rat, the biker and his girl—have settled for a solitary idea of freedom. Without ever saying it, they seem to believe that freedom is despoiled by other people. It's the same belief that sends John Wayne's outlaw, the Ringo Kid, riding away from the blessings of civilization at the end of John Ford's *Stagecoach*. But at least Ringo has Claire Trevor's Dallas to keep him company. Kowalski is so solitary that for him freedom is even despoiled by having too much time alone to wallow in his own thoughts and memories. Speed and motion are the answer. In *Vanishing Point*, Kowalski tears through a land that takes no notice of him—a land that, heading west as fast as he can, he will soon reach the end of. So, for

Kowalski, America becomes a state of mind that he aims to reach through . . .

SPEED

"The last American hero to whom speed means freedom of the soul." That's how Super Soul (Cleavon Little), the blind DJ who seems to have a sixth sense for what Kowalski is doing and thinking, mythologizes the driver. Kowalski is the descendant of the pioneers, "the last beautiful free soul." But, unlike the pioneers, Kowalski doesn't see the land. He's totally focused on the road ahead, and Barry Newman, with his mop of curly black hair and meaty nose, looks just handsome enough to lift him above being a regular schmo. He stops short of leading-man pretty, giving an eloquent though almost completely silent performance, wearing a dreamy near-smile for much of the movie. Kowalski is so settled into his driver's groove that when a motorcycle cop pulls up alongside him to cite him for speeding, you can see him shake himself out of the reverie he's fallen into. The only things Kowalski ingests in the movie are a Coke, a few cigarettes, and the uppers that keep him going—and he doesn't even wait for water to wash those down. He stops for gas or when he's lost in the desert. Even his clothes—a white shirt, brown vest, and jeans—seem to have been chosen for their lack of distraction.

The screenplay was written by the Cuban novelist and film critic Guillermo Cabrera Infante under the (completely ginchy) pseudonym Guillermo Cain. It's no slight to Infante to speculate that if the finished film is faithful to his script, it's hard to imagine it was more than a series of lyrical notes for a film to begin with.

Vanishing Point is hot-rod movie as tone poem, a picture about speed as Zen state, for both the hero and the audience. *Vanishing Point* wants to get us off on pure movement, but that movement, shown in long shots accompanied by the rev of the Challenger's engine, stretches time out instead of feeding our adrenaline.

That is a very odd thing for a picture that must have been sold to Twentieth Century-Fox as an exploitation movie that would lure in not just the gearheads and action fans but the counterculture moviegoers who had turned out for *Easy Rider*, the ones eager to celebrate Kowalski in just the terms Super Soul paints him. That the movie wasn't what anyone would imagine from that description may explain why Fox, which had no faith in it, released *Vanishing Point* via the neighborhood and drive-in route—and why it must have confounded Fox when it became a hit. And it *is* confounding. There's no doubting the movie's cool, but nobody expects a drive-in movie to be meditative, or for audiences to get excited about a meditative movie. That *Vanishing Point* was a critical and commercial hit overseas the Fox execs could probably put down to European perversity. Richard C. Sarafian isn't interested in making a demolition derby. Neither Kowalski nor the cops chasing him kill or injure anyone. Cars are run off the road, but there are no pileups or fiery crashes. When some schmuck in a Jaguar ends up in a creek after challenging Kowalski to a race, Kowalski, even with the sirens wailing in the background, gets out of the car to make sure the small-timer is okay.

The freaks-versus-straights tension that made *Easy Rider* a hit is present in *Vanishing Point*, but Kowalski has moved beyond it. He aspires to a state of oblivion, all memory and thought subsumed by the pure sensation of speed, his focus on the few yards of road in front of him. Even when those pursuing cops intrude on Kowalski's meditative hot-rodding, the movie doesn't take on any particular urgency. If *Vanishing Point* has any true heir in American cinema, it's not revved-up cheapies like *Gone in 60 Seconds* or the plusher *Fast and Furious* series but Vincent Gallo's notorious *The Brown Bunny*. Most of that movie is seen through a dirty or rain-streaked windshield as Gallo, playing a former motorcycle racer, drives from New Hampshire to Los Angeles. *The Brown Bunny* gives you the view you get from behind the wheel on a long drive, green highway signs looming overhead, rain turning everything into a soft blur. The rare moments of rest in motels and hotels have what Truman Capote once referred to as the "white silence" of such places, the sense of temporary refuge cradled like a caesura between days of travel.

There's never any doubt that Kowalski can outrun the cops. That's not just a matter of skill. This is the movies and there's no way someone with Barry Newman's casual cool is going to be bested by a bunch of aspiring good ol' boys with Dry Look haircuts and Smokey the Bear hats. The question the movie asks is: Can he outrun himself?

HISTORY

In the course of their pursuit, the authorities manage to discover that Kowalski was a professional race-car driver and a decorated war veteran wounded in the Mekong Delta though later given a dishonorable discharge. True to the mysterious nature of the character, the movie never tells us why. In one of Kowalski's flashbacks, which occasionally interrupt the narrative, we find out Kowalski was a cop, and apparently a rebel cop. In one scene he stops his older partner from raping a girl picked up on a drug charge. Later we see a headline proclaiming Kowalski a hero cop over a photo of him on courthouse steps. (The suggestion is that he was a whistle-blower.) But for all the bits and pieces, the cops find they can't discover Kowalski's first name.

Kowalski, with that one-name mystery, is clearly conceived as a symbolic construct, the straight arrow forced by the system to become a rebel. He could have been an enigmatic drag, a portentous counterculture version of Clint Eastwood's Man with No Name, if Barry Newman's affable, approachable physical presence didn't ground him, didn't make you trust him. The specifics of what Kowalski is trying to escape are suggested by the movie's flashbacks, but they matter less than the determination to escape.

The mostly unspoiled landscapes Kowalski speeds through are the kind always invoked to conjure our pioneer past. But *Vanishing Point*'s history isn't even history. The phrase "it's history" is a way of denying the very idea of history, of saying the past is dead and has no effect on the present or the future. The land we see in *Vanishing Point* is unmistakably present. The scant marks humans have left on it, those stark gas stations and diners, are already part of a past. But not the land itself. And so Kowalski's quest seems to be to merge with that land. And that is what leads the movie to . . .

THE FINISH LINE

You know what's going to happen from the beginning, when Sarafian takes his time setting up a shot of two bulldozers laying their shovels cheek to cheek on the asphalt and Kowalski heading straight towards them. And yet, unlike the end of *Easy Rider*, with its two biker heroes sacrificed for the sins of redneck America, there's no nihilism in this ending. What seems most discordant, the smile on Kowalski's face as he floors the Challenger to meet those bulldozers head-on, is the most fitting. The movies of this era frequently end with the heroes dead, and even if the plot reasons for their deaths aren't fully explicable, the deaths still made sense. The vibe in the air is hopelessness and futility, not triumph.

It's hard to say, exactly, why *Vanishing Point*—a movie that ends with a suicide—doesn't feel hopeless, even if that ending stuns you into silence. Whatever the reasons, it has to do with Barry Newman's smile. It's the smile that comes from having eluded expectation, memory, despair, from—just for a moment—doing what you want for no other reason than because you want to. Profound? No. Selfish? Maybe. But Sarafian manages to convey Kowalski's decision by pure sensation, and sensation is the means by which movies often articulate their emotional and psychological states. Kowalski's literal vanishing point is the shovels of the bulldozers he slams into. Beyond him, another vanishing point, America and the freedom it promises, once again recedes into the distance.

FAREWELL TO THE FIRST GOLDEN ERA:
CISCO PIKE

*Have you ever dreamed about a place you never really recall being to
before? A place that maybe only exists in your imagination? Someplace
far away, half-remembered when you wake up. When you were there,
though, you knew the language. You knew your way around. That
was the '60s. No. It wasn't that either. It was just '66 and early '67.
That's all it was.*

—PETER FONDA IN *THE LIMEY*

IN BILL NORTON'S *Cisco Pike* it's about 1970 or '71. In other words it's still
the '60s. Barely. This is a movie about the implosion of an era, specifically the part of the counterculture centered on the Los Angeles rock
'n' roll scene. And even rock 'n' roll seems to have taken its leave. The
song that opens the movie is Kris Kristofferson's "Loving Her Was
Easier" and the sound of the music is a retreat. When Kristofferson
sings the plain, devastating chorus, "*Lovin' her was easier than
anything I'll ever do again*," he's not just saying good-bye to a woman,
he's saying good-bye to whatever it was that made life bearable. There
is, in the song, as in much of country music, a deep acceptance of loss
and regret, and of the hard times ahead. That acceptance is the
acceptance of limits. It's the opposite of rock 'n' roll, which damns
limits even if pushing against those limits means damning yourself.
But as the counterculture collapsed in on itself, loss and regret and

37

acceptance were the feelings that, courtesy of country, had begun filtering into rock 'n' roll. In *Cisco Pike*, it's gotten so that when the characters wind up at the Troubadour one aimless night, the headliner is Waylon Jennings.

By the time Kristofferson took on the role of Cisco (his first lead; he'd had a small part the previous year in *The Last Movie*, Dennis Hopper's *film maudit*), a washed-up rock star pushed back into selling dope by a corrupt cop (Gene Hackman), his songs had already bridged the era's straight/freak divide. He'd written hits for C & W performers like Sammi Smith ("Help Me Make It Through the Night") and Ray Price (the countrypolitan treatment of "For the Good Times," which layered on strings and vibes), and for his former lover Janis Joplin (who had her only number one, posthumously, with "Me and Bobby McGee"). Even in an era when singer-songwriters as good as Carole King and as treacly as James Taylor were dominating rock, Kristofferson stood out. Cool enough for the rock 'n' roll crowd but with his true allegiance to country and western, this Rhodes scholar turned Nashville tunesmith turned laid-back cowboy-stud troubadour was a singular character. By his second album, 1971's *The Silver Tongued Devil and I* (on the cover of which he appears in character as Cisco), Kristofferson was already stoking his own legend. In the prologue to "The Pilgrim, Chapter 33," Kristofferson claims the song was inspired by everyone from Dennis Hopper to Johnny Cash to Ramblin' Jack Elliott. That long list of indebtedness, delivered in Kristofferson's soon-to-be trademark bedroom croak, couldn't disguise that the song was about him. The song is a rueful/sentimental celebration of the beautiful-loser myth and when Kristofferson appears before us in the opening scene of *Cisco Pike*, a hot young star playing a has-been, he's well on his way to being the incarnation of that myth.

In the opening shots, Cisco makes his way through a deserted section of Venice Beach that could come right out of Kristofferson's song "Sunday Mornin' Comin Down," the ramshackle houses suggesting the ramshackle lives inside. Cisco, "in his jacket and his jeans," looks like that song's now cruelly sober boozer, trampling the shards of his past under his boots like the broken bottles from last night's bender littering the sidewalk. In his hands, Cisco carries the emblem of his past, a battered acoustic guitar he's taking to the local music shop to sell.

"I'm getting back in the music business," Cisco tells the owner (played by that sly and wonderful actor Roscoe Lee Browne), an old acquaintance whose happiness at seeing Cisco after so long can't disguise his sadness at seeing him so obviously down and out. It's a measure of the man's kindness that he acts as if he believes Cisco, and a measure of his decency that he refuses to buy the instrument. "This is *your* guitar, Cisco," he tells him with a firm, rueful smile, sending him on his way, hoping for a good outcome but not expecting it. For the next ninety-four minutes, this is close to the only act of kindness we'll see.

What follows is a series of slights, threats, disappointments, and betrayals, all of them stemming from the squeeze that Hackman's dirty cop Holland is putting on Cisco. Holland has busted Cisco for dealing, twice, and the second charge, still hanging over Cisco's head, could send Cisco to the pen for a three-to-five stretch. Holland promises to make the charge go away—if Cisco will unload the high-grade grass he's stolen from a dealer. It's a heavy inventory, a hundred keys, and Holland gives Cisco just three days to do it. He's got a weekend to come up with ten grand for Holland or it's the slammer for sure.

On the Bantam paperback edition of the script that was issued to coincide with the movie's release, Norton (who has, at various times, been known as B. L. Norton, Bill Norton, Bill L. Norton), explained the genesis of the film by saying "I feel very strongly about the police, and Los Angeles, and the fact that nowadays we are all criminals. I mean it's hard to do anything without breaking laws. We are all criminals. We are all felons." The movie is a cruel illustration of Norton's supposition.

Were *Cisco Pike* operating via a standard noir setup, the movie's sense of dread would come from Cisco's struggle to unload the dope under the looming threat of Holland's deadline. But the task proves almost ridiculously easy. Norton gives us montages of Cisco dropping off his bundles at recording sessions and with doormen of upscale buildings, in a junkyard, a boatyard, at a commercial shoot. When Cisco informs his lawyer (Severn Darden) of the bind he's in, even this guy shows some interest in buying a key.

When Cisco drops into the recording session of his old crony Rex who's still hot on the charts (Rex is played to oblivious perfection by Doug Sahm, leader of the Tex-Mex outfit the Sir Douglas Quintet) hoping to get some encouragement about the tapes of new music he's sent, he finds that Rex isn't much interested in them but that he's real keen on getting Cisco to score him some of that *good* dope. In a matter of minutes Cisco finds himself dismissed with a hippie's version of noblesse oblige and handed over to Rex's manager (Allan Arbus, at his wiliest), a slick operator who tries to screw over Cisco on the price of a key.

The sequence is one indignity piled on top of another and it's central to the sense of dread that hangs over the movie, dread you can read on Kristofferson's face as Cisco keeps trying to present himself as a musician instead of a connection. Cisco wears the look of a man with a gun to his head forced to be a good sport. Like Jane

Fonda's Bree Daniels in *Klute*, told by her iron maiden of a shrink she should accept that she's successful as a call girl but not an actress, Cisco is finding exactly what he's valued for. And, like Bree, it galls him. But Bree and Cisco are opposites. The Jane Fonda of *Klute* has an exterior as hard and no-nonsense as Barbara Stanwyck in *Night Nurse* and *Baby Face*. But each indignity Bree endures registers as a jab at her insides. Kristofferson, clean shaven at this point, has a raw-boned boyishness. And he greets every moment that reminds him he's a has-been as if, behind that smooth skin, granite is sliding into place.

Most of the people Cisco encounters remember the gig that made him and his now-MIA partner Jesse famous, a '67 show at L.A.'s Shrine Auditorium. But that was nearly five years before and, in the time frame of the '60s, five years is forever. It's two and a half times longer than the two years it took to go from the Summer of Love to the Manson murders. And that brief but immense journey encompasses the blight that Norton is trying to convey here, the sweet, rotten smell of corruption that General Sternwood in *The Big Sleep* can smell in his orchids just at the moment they are in bloom.

In some ways, *Cisco Pike* is a West Coast cousin to Donald Cammell and Nicholas Roeg's *Performance* (1968, released 1970), the movie in which Mick Jagger, as a reclusive, nearly forgotten rock star hiding out in a decaying London mansion, confronts an East End gangster played by James Fox. *Cisco Pike* doesn't have *Performance*'s maddening, fragmented structure, its Borgesian illusion-and-reality games, or the sense of decay so palpable that it feels as if, to borrow a line from Dylan, the carpet, too, is crawling under you. But, like *Performance*, *Cisco Pike* is about a time and a place that's dead and hasn't got the good sense to fall over.

In the rock 'n' roll history of L.A., this era has been tradition-ally associated with anything but rot. It's the era of the burgeoning Southern California sound, the folkish, countryish music coming from Laurel Canyon, typified by the likes of Joni Mitchell, Crosby, Stills & Nash, and eventually the horror that is the Eagles. At the bottom of much of this music, even the best of it, was a smug, self-satisfied hippie domesticity (*"Our house is a very, very, very fine house"* or *"the sun poured in like butterscotch and stuck to my all my senses"*).

This wasn't the earned domesticity of Bob Dylan's *Nashville Skyline* or Van Morrison's *Tupelo Honey*, yearnings for tranquility from artists who had wrung themselves inside out musically and emotionally. With a few exceptions (Mitchell's icky "Woodstock," and the outraged and mournful Kent State protest "Ohio," which said more about the sensibility of its writer Neil Young than about CSN, who he recorded it with) there were no songs about communal feeling, or communal politics. Southern California rock may have had its roots in the sound of bands like the Byrds and Buffalo Springfield. Its sensibility, though, was an implicit rejection of the shared utopian vision of the '60s that had existed in those bands, in the harmonies of the Byrds (a far cry from CSN's shrill attempts at harmony) and the sound of Roger McGuinn's chiming guitars, and in the calm, steady defiance of Buffalo Springfield's "For What It's Worth." The Byrds grasped the implosion of the '60s dream before any of these performers. Past their hit-making days, the band opened 1968 by releasing, in January, *The Notorious Byrd Brothers*. The album can now be heard as an advance action against the horrors that year was to hold, a hunkering down that took its cue from a line in the album's cover of Gerry Goffin and Carole King's "Goin' Back," *"Thinking young and growing older is no sin."*

This was music about trying to hold on to some sense that it was possible to live your life in the way you chose at a time when it was coming to seem as if sin of one kind or another were the only option. (Greil Marcus would later say the album "caught the secret remorse of late sixties rebellion like nothing else.")

The title *The Notorious Byrd Brothers* suggests the rock 'n' roll group as western outlaws. If that was the image Kristofferson created for himself, it's an image that Bill Norton uses ironically. Cisco is less an outlaw among the straights he encounters than among the freaks. Not out of his twenties, he's a veteran from a utopian era at loose ends in a time that has maintained the trappings of that earlier period but turned inward. Cisco has fallen off the merry-go-round, but he's among people still on their painted ponies who don't deign to notice—or care—that he's bumped his ass. There's a discrepancy between Cisco's youth and the hard miles already on him. Kristofferson, not yet having grown the beard that, along with his crooning creak, would be the crowning glory of his sexy swagger, has a smooth, almost baby face. (In a 1971 BBC performance with his band, a few months after shooting *Cisco Pike*, a bearded Kristofferson, already sprouting a few grey hairs, seems to have grown into the heartache and regret of his songs.) Cisco is hip to the perfidy of the scuzzy milieu he lives in but he's also unprotected, susceptible not just to Holland's threat but to the users around him, the ones who'll be able to move on with no wounds to show. Among the most vivid of these is the Warhol "superstar" Viva as a society girl whose decadence is being bankrolled by her infirm daddy. Viva isn't an actress. She delivers her lines in a flatlined whine and her big spacey peepers cast a bored eye on everything around her. Viva is a presence in the process of becoming an absence, checked out but still nattering on. The social register freak she's playing here makes the scene in a spiffy convertible accompanied by her own private girl toy, an up-for-anything young tagalong, all toothy eagerness and blond shag who, as played by Joy Bang, looks as if Brian Jones had come back as a baby whore. (Cisco isn't in such a hurry to sell his dope that he passes up the offer to fall into the feathers with the both of them.) Viva's opposite is Cisco's old partner, Jesse, played by Harry Dean Stanton (billed as H. D. Stanton) with a touching, deferential courtliness. Even at the age of thirty-five, Stanton's weary lined face showed every mile he'd traveled. Jesse shows up at Cisco's place, strung out on heroin but such a gentlemen that he still presents a bouquet to Cisco's girlfriend (Karen Black in a fairly disposable role) when she walks in on him lolling bare-assed in the bathtub. He's Cisco's Dorian Gray, the picture of what lies in store for Cisco, and the way Stanton plays Jesse—a worn-out slipper kept around because he's more familiar than useful—carries a sting.

Despite the fact that this is a counterculture movie with a corrupt cop putting the screws to the hero, Norton doesn't use Holland as a cardboard stand-in for The Man. For such an unshowy actor, Hackman has always had an odd ability to seem at home in the skin of put-on artists, men who do their best to keep their enemies off balance. It's that quality, hidden by a wardrobe that looks as if it came straight from Sears, that makes Holland seem so dangerous. He's a crooked son of a bitch pretending to be a straight arrow. It's not just the cockiness of a dirty cop that makes Holland such a tricky adversary; it's that his dirty dealings carry with them a trace of sadism. It's desperation that pushes him to put the screws to Cisco, but we can see that he enjoys it. Holland isn't given enough screen time (Hackman is top billed but it's a supporting role) for Norton to explore the ways in which he's as trapped as

Cisco. But it's a mark of how smart *Cisco Pike* is about its era, of the cold eye it turns on the milieu and how it resists romanticization, that the movie is able to acknowledge Holland's trap.

This is a movie in which the scuff marks are as much psychic as physical. As shot by Vilis Lapenieks, *Cisco Pike* is, like *Aloha, Bobby and Rose* and *Hickey & Boggs*, one of those movies that is at home with a street-level view of Los Angeles. The majority of the movie takes place around Venice Beach, which looks less like a charmingly down-at-the-heels place for artists and nonconformists than a bolt-hole. Cisco's place is down a narrow alleyway, and the furnishings that would have seemed so eccentric and whimsical a few years before—scavenged antiques and old-time posters—look like the scraps he's been able to salvage wherever he can, less style than desperation. A whiff of mustiness seems to accompany the California sunshine in this movie, in the dives as well as in the better-appointed dwellings. The lives we see have been stunted, but not many have the impetus to try and get out alive.

"Doc wondered how many people he knew had been caught out tonight in this fog," writes Thomas Pynchon in the last passages of his novel *Inherent Vice*, his great elegy for the '60s. Doc is Pynchon's private-eye hero, Doc Sportello, who wanders through this stoner *Big Sleep*, into one labyrinthine situation after another, struggling (along with us) to comprehend its parameters. Pynchon's novel is a work of profound melancholy. The author is saying good-bye to a time that, for all its foolishness and capacity for self-destructiveness, made many people feel freer than they have ever felt, made them feel their lives were their own to determine. Pynchon the paranoid humanist understands there will always be forces that will do whatever they can to shut down that type of freedom. And he understands the hardness of settling for less once you've experienced that sort of freedom. It's the seemingly untra-versible distance from Jim Morrison demanding *"We want the world and we want it . . . now!"* to Kristofferson begging *"Help me make it through the night."* The beauty and the backbreaking grace Pynchon holds open as a possibility is that even tyranny does not excuse us from acting like human beings. His message is the same one with which Prince opens "Let's Go Crazy": *"Dearly beloved, we are gathered here today to get through this thing called life."*

Norton, a pessimist, and without the luxury Pynchon had of looking back on the era, can't summon any of the author's rueful nostalgia. The collapse Norton was trying to chronicle as it was happening cancels out the expansive joy that had once existed. The only way Cisco can get out alive is to escape, and even though Norton allows him to escape at a time when most movie antiheros were dead by the time the credits rolled, this hard, despairing film treats even Cisco's survival as a kind of pessimism. In the last shots Cisco, in his battered old car, makes his way through rural California to God knows where.

In some ways Cisco is escaping the future Kristofferson lived out in movies to come, most notably the wreck of a rock star he played so touchingly in the appalling Barbra Streisand version of *A Star Is Born.* Standing before a screaming stadium of fans (one thing the film did very well was capture the Dionysian frenzy of '70s arena shows), Kristofferson looks out and asks, "Are you a figment of my imagination, or am I one of yours?" A kinder fate has befallen the gentle journeyman lothario Blackie Buck, whom Kristofferson plays in Alan Rudolph's shaggy-dog road comedy *Songwriter.* Blackie's life is spent on a tour bus, shuttling between one-night stands, some onstage and some in the hotels after. He's a happy hedonist and Kristofferson—still as he was in *A Star Is Born,* wearing shirts as no

more than props, peekaboo draping for his bare muscled chest—
seems more sustained by the road than battered by it.

But the end of *Cisco Pike* shuts down even that modest possibility. The worry on Kristofferson's face as he drives with his few
possessions in a car that looks as if it could give out at any time
negates the promise and lure of the open road. It's the look of a man
in the midst of escape who may never stop worrying that he hasn't
run far enough away.

BEBOP/SILENCE: *HICKEY & BOGGS*

AT FIRST THE sound they made was jazz. Two hipsters, effortlessly tuned in to each other, familiar with each other's rhythms, elisions, phrasing, each so confident he didn't feel the need to outdo his partner. And they were partners. When the white guy was offered the gig, he made it clear he wouldn't take it if the black guy was going to be only a sideman. Partners. That's how it was going to be. Each distinct enough to be a soloist and both secure enough to duet. Sounding like put-on artists to whoever was listening, they talked to each other as only two men committed to playfulness could talk, finding a way to say what was important without saying it. Keeping their cool, keeping their style no matter what tempo changes got thrown at them, was as much a matter of pride as being turned out in the coolest threads. And there was never any of that jive about *Is the white guy hip enough to play with the black guy?* The question always was *Were we hip enough to hear them?*

Nearly fifty years after it premiered on NBC in September 1965, *I Spy* remains television's oasis of cool. There have been smarter shows, deeper shows, more daring shows, shows that played with the medium. But there's been nothing like the effortless cool embodied by Robert Culp and Bill Cosby playing two spies traveling the world under the guise of a tennis pro and his trainer. *I Spy* was famous for being shot in exotic locales, but the glimpses of those lands couldn't disguise the cardboard studio-set quality of the exposition scenes. And unlike another spy show that was a hit at the same time, the British import *The Avengers*, *I Spy* didn't have particularly clever plots or the sci-fi comic-book weirdness of the adventures in which John Steed and Emma Peel found themselves each week. Steed and Peel epitomized British reserve and dry wit retrofitted for '60s mod. Culp's Kelly Robinson and Cosby's Alexander Scott ("Scotty") were American smartasses who dug jazz, European tailoring, the luxe surroundings you might see in one of those "What Sort of Man Reads *Playboy*?" ads. They also never broke a sweat.

Culp had worked on the New York stage and as the lead in a Western series called *Trackdown*. Early on he showed an interest in writing and directing. By the time *I Spy* went off the air after three seasons, he'd written seven episodes.

Cosby had come up through nightclubs and began releasing comedy LPs, all of them best sellers, in 1964, although he was always less a stand-up comic than a humorist. There were jokes in his act, but mostly you heard stories, long stories about family life or being a kid growing up in a city neighborhood, with characters who were both strange and instantly believable. At times, listening to Cosby, you could start to imagine that the oddballs who populated the banks of Twain's Mississippi had spawned descendants in inner-city Philadelphia. (Pudd'nhead Wilson meet Old Weird Harold. You two have a lot to talk about.) It was after seeing Cosby at a nightclub gig that the actor turned producer Sheldon Leonard, veteran of dozens of tough-guy movie roles, abandoned the idea of making Scotty an older mentor to Kelly and instead cast Cosby who had never before acted. Culp later said of the partnership, "We met and decided that we liked each other. Everything else for me and Bill took second position to that. Both of us had total trust in each other."

That trust seems to be where their rapport came from. Culp
later claimed that the seven episodes he wrote over the show's three-
year run were the only scripts filmed as written. Watch almost any
scene between him and Cosby and you can believe that's not just a
scenarist's boast. "We almost had our own language and our own
way of connecting, sometimes without saying anything," said
Cosby after Culp's death in 2010. It would be next to impossible to
write for two actors who've achieved that. Their scenes raised
ad-libbing to the level of telepathy. The dialogue is sometimes so
softly spoken that you have to lean in to hear what they're saying.
And the lead-ins are never predictable. In one episode, imprisoned
and watched over by a Spanish guard who has a guitar along
with his rifle, Kelly initiates a gambit to break out. Slouched against
the wall of the cell, seemingly engaged in looking at something
on the floor, he says to Scotty just what you might expect of
someone in that situation: "Listen," Kelly begins. "You, uh . . . dig
flamenco?"

"Yeah," answers Scotty earnestly, fiddling with his hat as
if there is nothing weird about this sudden cultural inquiry, as if
nothing could be more important at that moment than conveying
his respect for the artistry of the Spanish guitar.

"Yeah, great . . . 'S beautiful," Kelly says, almost to himself.
And then, bright and clear and direct, "Go tell him."

"What?" asks Scotty, just a tad befuddled.

"Go tell him," says Kelly, drawing out the words, warming to
the idea hatching in his brain, "that you love his work . . . G'head."
And, that said, he slouches back against the wall, enjoying his
smoke.

Did I mention that Boris Karloff is standing by while all this
unfolds?

It ends, of course, with Scotty, whom Kelly has convinced the guard is a student of Segovia, using the guitar to bash their captor over the head. But think how a scene like this is usually written and played ("Listen, I've got an idea. If you can make him believe you're a student of flamenco . . .") and the oddball hipness of what Culp and Cosby do, their determination to avoid the straight course because the zigzag one is more fun, seems much more the point of the scene than advancing the plot. Style is paramount. As is trusting that no matter what wiggy course your partner charts for you, he's going to land the both of you just where you need to be.

What we see in Culp and Cosby's partnership isn't just an attitude or a put-on but an ethics of professionalism and respect and a belief that how you carry yourself and how you present yourself says everything about your capability and competence. Everything you needed to know about the show's casual elegance could be seen in the white dress shirts Culp wore during the first season. With their three-button barrel cuffs (at a time when two buttons was thought to be fashion forward) and a masterpiece of a collar combining, as it did, button-down tabs with a soft, rolled Mr. B neck (as designed and worn by Billy Eckstine), the shirts mixed the precision of Ivy League tailoring with the casual cool of swinger chic. Those shirts seemed like summation of the loopy professionalism with which Kelly and Scotty approached their job, and Culp and Cosby their roles.

The chemistry between Culp and Cosby was the reason the show was so popular. That equal footing between a white man and a black man was also the reason the show was not shown on some southern NBC affiliates. It's become common to cite race as the show's enduring significance, which is an ironic legacy for a show that made the decision not to talk about race. "Our statement was a nonstatement," Culp said. The obvious—Cosby was the first black actor hired for a leading role on an American TV series who wasn't expected to shuck and jive—didn't need to be said. So the real subject of the show became two actors who trusted each other playing two characters who trusted each other. *I Spy* and its stars were content to let that trust speak for itself. Also implicit but left unsaid was that the show's foreign locations were places where a black American didn't, for instance, have trouble getting served in a restaurant or taking a room in a good hotel—or trouble sharing the room with his white friend if he wished to.

It may be foolhardy to look for significance in coincidence. But sometimes chance provides its own kind of melancholy music, and it's hard to ignore that *I Spy* premiered six months after the Memphis-to-Montgomery march, the pinnacle of the civil rights movement, and aired its last episode a little over a week after Martin Luther King Jr. was murdered. In other words, this story of a part-nership conducted with an ease that was proving so hard to achieve in real life came just at the time when the heady victories of the previous nine years—the Montgomery bus boycott; the Civil Rights Act of 1964; the Selma–Montgomery march; the 1965 Voting Rights Bill—were giving way to an America that would shortly retreat from the desire to rectify its sins and the determination those victories had shown to do just that. "It is not just Negroes," President Lyndon Johnson said in his March 1965 address to Congress in support of the Voting Rights Act, "but really it is all of us, who must overcome the crippling legacy of bigotry and injustice," before echoing the words of the civil rights movement in a phrase that segregationists felt like a knife in their hearts: "And we shall overcome."

The years that followed the triumphs of the civil rights movement saw the splintering of the alliances that movement had fostered across races and the ascendant separatism of the emerging Black Power movement. Even before Dr. King's murder there was a growing, often flip dismissal of his insistence on nonviolence as utopian or, worse, Tomming. The methods of the Black Panthers and other groups, turning the brutality of White Power into a self-fulfilling prophecy by pushing authorities to confrontations the authorities were bound to win, could be summed up by the title of Huey Newton's book, *Revolutionary Suicide*. The new reality of the time was a world that seemed to say to people *You're on your own*.

That's the world of the bitter private-eye movie *Hickey & Boggs* in which Culp and Cosby reunited four years after *I Spy* went off the air. The movie's dour silences, its disappointments, barely articulated because that would mean admitting them, are haunted by the memory of the prankish music that Culp and Cosby made together on *I Spy*. Culp, directing the only theatrical movie he ever got the chance to make, wanted to work with his old partner, and he must have hoped the pairing would bring in the audiences who remembered *I Spy* with pleasure. But the few movie-goers who did show up must have wondered just what the hell they were watching. The movie seemed to come out of nowhere and soon returned there.

It's not just the memory of the chemistry the two stars had in *I Spy* that haunts *Hickey & Boggs*. It's that series' dream-vacation locales, the elegant clothes, the sports cars, the whole hip attitude to danger that said risking your life was a gas. And while there was never any doubt Kelly and Scotty were heroes, *Hickey & Boggs* doesn't even provide that assurance. In Walter Hill's script—written three years before his 1975 directing debut, *Hard Times*—Hickey and Boggs are two down-and-out Los Angeles PIs hired by a mob associate (a gaudy homosexual caricature who's an implied child molester—one of the movie's few missteps) to locate the courier who's absconded with the loot she'd been dispatched to deliver to a money launderer. Their employer claims the woman is a missing girlfriend, but he doesn't really expect the detectives to believe him, and doesn't care if they do. He knows these two are the type of low-renters who won't ask many questions. The sting of the movie is that Hickey and Boggs (Cosby and Culp, respectively) know that about themselves. They understand that this kind of job is how low they've sunk, errand boys for the mob but too far in the hole to be able to turn down any business and, on some level, believing that's the sort of low-rent assignment they deserve.

Hickey & Boggs is determinedly drab. Every wall looks like it needs a paint job, every window is streaked with grime. There are shots of cigarette butts on dirty, buckled linoleum floors. Some indistinguishable swath of the L.A. freeway rushes by Al Hickey's front yard. Inside, swatches of wallpaper have been ripped away from the walls, there's barely enough light to see, and every conversation, no matter how painful (Hickey is separated from his wife, who is living in the house) is conducted to the ever-present sound of traffic.

Frank Boggs has a house but we never see it. He floats between the office he shares with Hickey, where the phone has been turned off for nonpayment and he sometimes entertains a whore (we see her arm reaching for the twenty he lays atop her ratty fur), and the dark interior of the run-down bar where he regularly gets soused while watching the fights or the football game on the black-and-white set that sits next to a sign telling patrons that beer is available for takeout.

Hickey and Boggs wear rumpled, ill-fitting clothes that look like they haven't seen the inside of a dry cleaner's in ages. (In some scenes you can see stains on Hickey's green sports jacket and the sweat coming through their white dress shirts.) Their cars are dusty old junkers neither can be sure will start up again every time they kill the engine.

Raymond Chandler had imbued even the sleazy parts of Los Angeles with a sinister allure and Philip Marlowe's detective work with a quixotic romanticism. In *Hickey & Boggs*, L.A. looks on its last legs, the kind of decaying city where the Greyhound station would be the brightest spot in town. It's a street-level view of the city, what you see driving or walking, not the view from the high-rises springing up all over town. The partners' office is round the back of an ancient brick building next to the rear door of a shoe store that doesn't look as if anyone ever goes in. But no one ever seems to be anywhere in this Los Angeles. This is a noir that takes place mostly in daylight, and yet, from scene to scene, it feels almost as empty as any nighttime street. All the locations are in run-down, nearly deserted parts of the city, an elephant's grave-yard of urban life. By the time the movie climaxes on a deserted stretch of beach, you barely notice the Pacific rolling in, and the sun shining through what looks like the only clean air in the movie. You feel as beat out as Hickey, dropping to his knees in the sand. He and Boggs seem so stunned they made it to the end of the case that they can barely take notice of the bodies all around them. They can only mutter that "nobody came . . . nobody cares."

Culp carries the thriller plot to its conclusion, but apart from a few crisply directed ambush scenes it has no urgency. That, I think, is a deliberate move on Culp's part—and a smart one. Even if Hickey and Boggs manage to retrieve the money and claim the reward that the hoods are offering for its return—money that could get them free and clear of their debts—nothing much is going to change for them. It's a bitter joke that they survive the final gun battle. They're not even crucial to the plot, not even heroes in their own movie. "The only thing you can do is goddamn try to even it up," Boggs says to Hickey during the lowest point of their investigation. But even that hardnosed view is too romantic for Hickey, who, at one point, tells his partner, "There's nothing left to this profession, it's all over. It's not about anything." Hickey knows in his gut that neither he nor Boggs are, like Philip Marlowe, the man who must go down the city's mean streets; or, like Ross Macdonald's Lew Archer, someone who sets out to restore what decency he can after intolerable secrets have come to the surface.

So instead of a making a thriller, Culp makes *Hickey & Boggs* a movie about the stasis—financial, professional, spiritual—of these two deeply unhappy, disconnected men. There are few clues to their past. At one point Boggs asks Hickey, "You ever kill anybody . . . in the U.S.?" and we can guess that somewhere along the way, maybe in the Army, these two met, bonded over shared experience, turned to private-eye work—and to each other's company—as a way to make a living without having to explain themselves to a world of people who hadn't been through what they had. *Hickey & Boggs* is about the moment when that kind of camaraderie is no longer enough. The interplay that began on *I Spy* is as much an intuitive marvel as ever. But this time the banter is less about the trust of this partnership than the irritability that comes from knowing your partner too well. "I'm going in the tank tonight, I think," Boggs, who's a drunk, says in an early scene, heading back inside the bar they've just exited. "Yeah," says Hickey, not even looking at his partner, having seen him set off on too many nights like this. These two have had it with each other, with having to drive crummy cars and wear uncomfortable "professional" clothes and scrimp to pay for their rat hole of an office and eat their lunch at shabby chili-dog stands. They've also had it with themselves but know it's safer to be annoyed with the other guy than to give in to the self-disgust they feel. There was a moment in the debut episode of *I Spy* where someone challenged Kelly by asking him who he thought he was. "He knows who he is," Scotty said, and it seemed the highest compliment he could give his partner. Both Hickey and Boggs know who they are, and they don't like what they know.

Actors' past roles are part of the history they bring to the screen. It's why it can be a shock when an actor departs from the persona they've established: when Henry Fonda turns into a stone killer in *Once Upon a Time in the West* or Steve Martin into a song-and-dance man in *Pennies from Heaven*. *I Spy* emanated from the good intentions that the civil rights movement had been able to make into concrete gains for ten amazing years. *Hickey & Boggs* is part of a moment when those good intentions had gone into retreat, when the very idea of a unifying spirit or movement was foreign to the fabric of American life. And so, while Culp and Cosby play off each other as beautifully as ever (to express bitterness rather than delight), we are watching two men who are essentially alone.

Culp does a very difficult thing for a star-director, let alone a first-timer: He doesn't protect himself from looking weak. When Boggs takes slugs from the fifth of Dewar's he keeps in the office filing cabinet, Culp makes it look like the bottle is swallowing bits of him. Boggs is the closest the movie comes to a romantic PI with a code. He believes in seeing the case through, and he has chival-rous impulses: When his ex-wife leaves her rich boyfriend, he prevails on a club owner to give her back her old job as a stripper. But Culp shows just how brittle a shell even that sliver of romanti-cism is. In his best scene, he sits drunk in a strip club waiting for his wife to come on. She comes out and does her show right in front of him, not even disguising the fact that she's taunting him for what he can never have, telling him, "Eat your heart out." Culp is more naked than she is. In the midst of the scene, he gives himself a close-up that is one of the moments when an actor appears totally exposed before us but still in control. You see the suggestion of tears forming in his eyes and, in contrast, a sick smile on his face as if, despite the humiliation he's enduring, he has to show this woman he's proud of her. It's the kind of moment that makes you want to turn away except that it would be a disservice to the bravery of the actor in front of you.

Cosby has a scene that's even better—amazing, really— although even as you're watching it you're aware that it's built on a perversity: a natural-born talker made to convey everything through silence. Finally convincing his wife to come back to him for a night, Hickey arranges to meet her at his apartment only to arrive and find that the mob has murdered her. After the funeral, Boggs catches up with him at the bar, where Hickey is occupying his usual stool. The scene that unfolds over four and a half minutes, an eternity in screen time, is an act of generosity on the part of Culp as director and actor. Even though he has every line in the scene, everything he does is to focus attention on Cosby. Boggs is trying to convince Hickey that the time has come for them to act. But no matter what tack he takes—it's time to close the case; it's time to avenge Hickey's wife; it's time Hickey put his wife's death behind him and got on with things—the more ineffectual he makes himself. He starts by asking Hickey, "You all right?" and when there's no response, he says, "Good," and that one word tells you that even though Hickey is silent, it's Boggs who isn't listening—or trying to ignore what's so plain. Paying no attention to Hickey's shell shock, Boggs goes on laying out the details of the case, trying to talk Hickey off that bar stool. It's incredibly callous. Boggs wants the reward money, he's got to have it, and he needs his partner's help.

Boggs tries everything, even saying to Hickey, "Just because you can't get this dumb, stupid, pitiful bitch out of your guts." It's horrendous, and yet you feel him trying to reach Hickey and trying in the only way he knows how: by talking to him, by not allowing Hickey to seal himself off. When, in disgust, Boggs makes to leave, he can't get through the door. And so he's drawn back to his bar stool, trapped as surely as one of Beckett's tramps.

Amazing as Culp is, Cosby surpasses it. It's the type of acting that would only be possible on screen, only possible with the intimacy of the camera, and yet I know of no other screen moment like it. Cosby makes Hickey's silence a reproach. He simply sits there, unmoving, looking down at the bar, distant and yet so present, you can tell that every imprecation from Boggs is like a paper cut across his fingers. He isn't visibly reacting but immersed in a febrile stillness that lets you know he's hearing every word. The payoff is Hickey getting up and leaving the bar so abruptly that Boggs has to rush to keep up with him. And yet its silence and stillness that remains.

That silence and stillness stand for the defeat at the heart of the movie, the simplest and most extreme expression of being immersed in a moment when you realize that nothing is going to get any better, that all of the excuses for why you should go on just sound like so much talk, when there's been too much lost and too many deaths and you'd just rather not try anymore. It would be a daring scene for an experienced director to pull off. That it's so superbly executed and so wounding makes it sadder that Culp never got a chance to direct another movie. Of course, Culp wouldn't have attempted it at all if he didn't believe that Cosby could pull it off. And so we arrive back at the mystery of trust and rapport. The final irony of *Hickey & Boggs* is that this movie about isolation and displacement is an affirmation of a real-life partnership. And one that now seems very rich, managing as it did, over the course of a tongue-in-cheek adventure series and a hard-edged, downbeat private-eye picture, to capture the mood of the country on the issue that we are forever being told it's time to have a conversation about. The partnership between Culp and Cosby did that by deciding not to have that conversation, which, we know, would have involved the inevitable platitudes and the smug self-satisfaction that comes with the pretense of having faced the tough issues and plastered them over with the facile smiley face of brotherhood. Which isn't to say that change didn't come, that it has never stopped coming. If we measure race by the possibility of change, then it says something about what's different now in American life that we have to remind ourselves that, in this partnership, the white guy wasn't just a sideman, either.

SHUT DOWN, VOLUME 2:
TWO-LANE BLACKTOP

IN MONTE HELLMAN'S *Two-Lane Blacktop* we're in a small-town North Carolina service station at what appears to be about six A.M. on a rainy Sunday morning. Maybe it's Saturday. The characters themselves aren't sure. These hot-rodders have pulled into the station to attend to a busted carburetor and it's just as well the place is closed. The mood of this drizzling dawn seeps into everything. Pretty soon they've drifted away from the task at hand to nip at a bottle, doze, wander the town. One or two people are visible on the street but something in the still, quiet air makes it feel like nothing's about to change. Saturday mornings in town give the promise of the bustle to come. Sunday never shakes off its sleepiness. Whatever day it is, in *Two-Lane Blacktop* it's always the rainy Sunday morning that you just can't shake.

You might expect a movie about rootless hot-rodders to be all Friday-night flash, the characters jacked up on speed and cockiness, street dragging for the glory and the cash before—inevitably—the cops come along to break things up.

Instead, *Two-Lane Blacktop*, which was written by the novelist and screenwriter Rudolph Wurlitzer, perches on the thin edge dividing deadened acceptance from profound despair.

Ostensibly, it's a movie about a cross-country race, the Driver (James Taylor) and the Mechanic (the Beach Boys' Dennis Wilson) and their souped-up primer-grey '55 Chevy sedan challenging

GTO (Warren Oates), the middle-aged hipster with his rainbow assortment of V-neck cashmere sweaters and tucked-in scarves, duds as slick as his canary-yellow Pontiac GTO. But none of them seem to have any more drive than the companion who gravitates between the three of them, a teenager on the road (seventeen-year-old Laurie Bird) who plunks herself down in the car of whoever will give her a ride. The Driver and the Mechanic look for street races when they need to make some bread to attend to their wheels. Mostly, they don't say much to anyone else or to each other. GTO talks endlessly to the hitchhikers he picks up, spinning out tales of where he's been and what he's done.

Except that none of them seem to be listening. *Two-Lane Blacktop* is a movie that fits the novelist Donna Tartt's description of novel writing: art "by the alone for the alone." The idea of seeing this movie with a crowd just seems wrong. The people who love this movie most—the ones I know include a critic who taped it off of USA Network's old late-night rock-and-movie showcase *Night Flight* and held on to her decaying VHS copy for years; and a young woman who, while prepping for a solo cross-country road trip, kept the DVD playing on her laptop like background music for a week—all seem to have encountered it by themselves and treat it as their own personal talisman. There are plenty of people who, by now, love *Two-Lane Blacktop*. (It wasn't always so.) But whatever it is in them that the movie speaks to, it's something as alone as the characters.

That's not how it was supposed to work. Universal, funding a production unit designed to produce "youth-oriented" pictures, expected *Two-Lane Blacktop* would capture the studio's share of the huge business that Columbia had done with *Easy Rider*. A month before its release, *Esquire* put a shot of a hitchhiking Laurie Bird on its cover with the announcement, "Read it first! Our nomination for movie of the year." Inside, the magazine printed Wurlitzer's screenplay in its entirety.

And the movie tanked.

A line from the Australian ad campaign, which wasn't enough to get it more than a single week at a tiny Melbourne art house, sums up everything that went wrong: "James Taylor—Rock Superstar of the '70s—in a saga of the road and the high speed scene where you can never go fast enough." The rock fans who might have gone to see James Taylor (riding the success of *Sweet Baby James*) or Dennis Wilson didn't know how to take the dour, monosyllabic, deliberately uningratiating countenance the two of them display for the whole movie. Action movie fans and racing fans, expecting excitement and suspense and lots of squealing rubber, found themselves watching a mood piece about a quartet of drifters that tosses away what semblance there is of a plot. Hellman, contractually obligated to bring the movie in at under two hours, pared down his three-and-a-half-hour rough cut by taking out most of the racing scenes and dwelling on the moments when the characters are sitting in the Chevy or some nondescript diner, usually silent and sullen, passing through this scrubby nowhere on their way to nowhere in particular. The counterculture crowd who wanted another *Easy Rider*, a bummer that flattered their sense of themselves as hippie Christs ready to be sacrificed for the sins of America, couldn't have been happy to find these two long-haired grease monkeys passing through small-town diners and gas stations and bars with nary a glance from the locals. Not a big-bellied sheriff or a rusty razor blade in sight.

Lew Wasserman, the head of Universal's parent company, MCA, reportedly hated the movie more than any other the company released under his leadership. As Kent Jones reports in his essay accompanying the Criterion edition of *Two-Lane Blacktop*, not only did it represent the new spirit of filmmaking that threatened the conventional Hollywood Wasserman understood, but the freaks and kids and hippies it was made for didn't even turn out to support it.

But Wasserman would have hated *Two-Lane Blacktop* even if it had made him money. The fact of the movie's existence, the fact that a major studio was even courting the counterculture, could only confirm that Hollywood, and the world, was changing beyond his ability to recognize it. Of course, the counterculture liked to be catered to as much as the old order it opposed, and it, too, had its own particular sentimentalities. And nothing in *Two-Lane Blacktop* caters to that sentimentality. The movie is marked not just by a quiet refusal to take sides but by the unspoken conviction that in a country of loners, sides can't exist. Hellman and Wurlitzer weren't preaching about what was wrong with America and what had to change. The Driver and the Mechanic, their names less enigmatic affectation than a gesture towards a kind of ordinariness, aren't rebels leading the way to a world where everyone throws off the shackles of routine. GTO, with his bachelor pad on wheels, whatever music he desires ready to play on the car stereo, and a selection of liquor and lowball glasses in the trunk, wasn't the square who had to get out of the way to make way for the new world. No one is demonized in this movie, no one glorified, no one vindicated. The characters drift into each other's orbit, but they do not form a community. When chance throws the Driver and GTO together in the same car and GTO starts to relate his story, the Driver cuts him off, telling him he doesn't care.

Two-Lane Blacktop has less in common with hot-rod and biker pictures than it does with Westerns and that genre's simultaneous desire to be part of and free of community. In *Two-Lane Blacktop* everyone is inextricably alone, wandering through an America where the notion of purpose has disappeared. The Driver and the Mechanic have the kind of expertise that would have earned them respect in a Howard Hawks movie, and the kind of stoic purposefulness that marks them as professionals. But except for a flicker of arrogance when they're challenged to prove just how fast the Chevy runs, there's no pleasure or pride in the victories. Just a determination to keep moving.

We learn nothing about where the Driver or the Mechanic come from, but Taylor and Wilson are playing off their public image—in Taylor's case, turning against it. The look on James Taylor's face on the cover of *Sweet Baby James*, the pensive, denim-shirted rock poet, said to generations of sensitive young women, *I'm damaged. Fuck me.* More than any other performer to emerge in the singer-songwriter boon of the early '70s, Taylor traded on folky vulnerability. In *Two-Lane Blacktop*, Taylor is so convincingly hard, so scowling and unfriendly, you begin to wonder whether his troubadour routine was just shtick. When some hapless weekend hot-rodder offers the Driver fifty bucks to find out just how fast the Chevy is, Taylor looks at the guy who's just made the measly offer and counters, "Make it three yards and you got an auto*mo*bile race, motherfucker." There are moments, when Taylor gives Bird a stray sideways look or tries to teach her to drive a stick shift, where he carries the suggestion of a man who might be ready to welcome human contact. In one sequence Taylor takes himself to a procession of bars in some nameless city, from run-down saloon to hotel cocktail lounge, while Wilson and Bird take the motel room for the night.

Taylor's Driver is as out of place in the saloon as in the hotel, too scruffy for the latter, too wrapped up in himself to partake of the bar's good-time vibes. Taylor sits hunched over, his arms folded protectively against his chest, looking as if he wouldn't mind talking if he could just find the right person, but also so forbidding he shuts everything out. There is the suggestion of a wound beneath the stoic exterior, and it's much more affecting than the soppy singer-songwriter confessionals that made Taylor's name.

In 1971, Dennis Wilson had none of Taylor's wimpy cachet. The Beach Boys, though still recording, had imploded amid Brian's breakdown and the charge of no longer being relevant at a time when rock 'n' roll had given way to the ponderous self-seriousness of "rock." And Wilson had floated into the darker side of the era, for a time giving the free run of his house to an aspiring musician named Charlie Manson and the entourage of girls and jackals who came with him.

Despite the critical talk that has from time to time tended to belittle the Beach Boys as hopelessly middle-class (the line went: Elvis' father worked in a factory; the Beach Boys' father owned one), the band's utopian Southern California vision of sun, girls, cars, good times, good buddies, and fun was as open as any pop vision to anyone who heard the music and whose soul said *Yes* in response. It was idealized but it wasn't a lie.

In *Two-Lane Blacktop*, the Beach Boys' music is a memory of another vision of freedom that's been shut down. Dennis Wilson has gone from being one of the Beach Boys to playing a character who might have been one of the kids who heard "Little Honda," "Fun, Fun, Fun," "I Get Around," "Little Deuce Coupe," and "Shut Down" on the radio and never got over them. And you look at this character, rugged and handsome in his beat-up jeans and white T-shirts, and see a harbinger of where he'll be at forty, in some crummy garage, maybe tooling around with a sports car on the weekend.

The memory of the freedom that Dennis Wilson stood for becomes, in the movie, another constriction. The sunniness of the Beach Boys is here replaced by grey skies, always promising rain or having just delivered it. Shooting inside the cars themselves, Hellman and his cinematographer Gregory Sandor reduce the open road to the view through grimy windows, from the backseat where the Girl tries to get comfortable even though the seat has been taken out to accommodate tools. Instead of the sound of revving engines, the soundtrack mainly offers the hum of tires on asphalt or the occasional patter of rain, characters so settled into themselves that their silences portend nothing.

Even the presence of a girl doesn't do much to break down that self-imposed solitude. What's affecting about Laurie Bird's untutored performance is that she is so young, still unformed (she's got a rosy-cheeked pout), but still shares the anomie and restlessness of the Driver and the Mechanic. There's no doubt she's paid her way for her travels with sex, but Hellman isn't interested in the cliché of the hot-to-trot hitchhiker. And with Taylor and Wilson, even when she offers, they barely seem to expect it. When she and the Mechanic settle down for the night in a motel room, they might as well be preparing to sack out after a long drive.

Hellman cuts away from the scene, returning to the motel only when Taylor, having relinquished the bed to them, comes back. And even then, the camera stays outside where Taylor will spend the night. It's a cutting image of loneliness, but you can't be sure it's any lonelier than what's going on in the room. The possible connections of sex or romance are remote in this movie. When GTO spins out swanky old-fashioned fantasies of taking Bird on a trip to New York, where they'll stay in a fancy hotel suite and paint the town, her only response is, "I don't want to go to New York."

She's not rejecting him. She'd have to consider him long enough to do that. As with almost every human interaction in the movie, this one takes place between two people on opposite sides of an untraversable distance.

For all the ways in which Taylor, Wilson, and Bird suit the movie's purposes, there's a way in which watching *Two-Lane Blacktop* without Warren Oates would be like trying to watch *Easy Rider* if it didn't have Jack Nicholson. Oates, the only one with acting experience, doesn't just provide the chops the other three lack, he sounds depths they don't come near. For an actor so identified with action movies, Oates, as in Sam Peckinpah's *Bring Me the Head of Alfredo Garcia*, often seemed like the most vulnerable person on screen. He is here, spinning out endless stories to the hitchhikers he picks up, stories of jobs, a family, a home, that sound as if they had drifted in from another life where possibilities still exist. The beauty of Oates's performance is the grace it confers on such a transparent man. GTO's tales of past glories are so clearly forgeries that the wry, devil-may-care grin he affects when telling them suggests how much it costs him to lie. It's as if the smile has to work its way past the deadweight of failure sitting in the middle of his chest. When a waitress approaches GTO in one more empty diner to take his order, he assumes the airs of a continental playboy as he says to her, "Champagne, caviar, chicken sandwiches under glass." Dismissing his jest with a ghost of a smile, he gives his real order, "Bacon, eggs over light, coffee, toast, jelly," his face settling into a grimace resigned to the immutable sameness of life. It's Oates who cracks the movie open, allowing all that's buried under the surface to pour out when he confesses to a sleeping Bird, "If I don't get grounded soon, I'm gonna go into orbit."

But where is there to go? The last minutes of the movie take in some lovely roadside greenery along the two-lane country highway.

But the cocktail music accompanying the images reminds us the ever-present danger of reducing this beauty to postcard phoniness. When GTO hangs out next to an old Coke freezer while his car is gassed up, he's as solitary as the man at the country-station pumps in Edward Hopper's painting *Gas* (1940). Hopper was the great painter of American solitude. In both his canvas and Hellman's movie, the primary colors stand out. But in Hopper's landscape, the red of the Mobil pumps is matched by the lush green of the pines and the fiery oranges of the browning leaves, all of it receding into the darkness of the surrounding woods. As painted by Hopper, this is still a civilization on the edge of unclaimed mystery. The trees that dot the flat, dusty landscape in which GTO takes his respite hold no mystery; they are sparse ornamentation on a denuded land where the only colors come not from nature but from commerce, from the yellow of Pontiac, the red of Coke, the dark green of Quaker State.

It's sadly fitting that *Two-Lane Blacktop* is now a movie of ghosts. Oates, dead of a heart attack at fifty-three. Wilson, dead eight months after Oates, accidentally drowned at thirty-nine. Bird, dead four years before either of them, a suicide at twenty-five.

James Taylor has never seen the film. Hellman, still working when he can, at eighty-four, spent the years after *Two-Lane Blacktop* occasionally getting to make films his way, reuniting with Oates for an adaptation of Charles Willeford's novel *Cockfighter* and for the odd, touching Western *China 9, Liberty 37*. But, also having to pay the bills, making the likes of *Silent Night, Deadly Night 3: Better Watch Out!* His last movie, the typically enigmatic and poetic *Road to Nowhere* (2010), ran out of money in the midst of production but still made it into theaters only to disappear quicker than *Two-Lane Blacktop* did during its initial run.

Of all the indignities suffered by *Two-Lane Blacktop*, perhaps the worst is the one detailed by Kent Jones in his Criterion essay. For years the final, essential images were cut from the studio print of the film. Perhaps, as Jones suggested, the studio projectionist didn't like a movie making it look like he screwed up.

It's another race, another grey indistinct day, another group of racing enthusiasts who the Driver and the Mechanic will soon leave behind. We're inside the car with Taylor. The sound is very far away—not as if the windows were shut but as if the world outside the car were underwater. The starter gives the signal and we watch from the camera's vantage point behind the Driver as he kicks the car into gear to pick up speed. But as he does, we notice that Taylor's hair has started to wave gently in mid-frame like seaweed, and we realize that, as the car accelerates, the film is slowing down. Slowing to the point where the image stops and, as if the print itself were stuck in the gate, begins to burn and disintegrate.

The ruins of the image fade to black; the credits roll silently. This is the beautiful and awful benediction Hellman lays on his movie and his characters, the only possible escape he can give them, the wish for speed rendered as a literal obliteration, and, as GTO predicted, the orbit that comes from not finding a place to be grounded.

A QUEEN WITHOUT A THRONE:
COFFY AND *FOXY BROWN*

HAS ANY MOVIE goddess ever done more with less than Pam Grier? With her stately bearing and voluptuous build, regal high cheek-bones, and proud, prominent nose, Grier is one of those rare performers, like Ava Gardner or Angelina Jolie, who seem to command the camera, and the adoration of the viewer, by natural right. But the money and resources of major Hollywood studios with the ability to give their stars lustrous settings in which to shine is just what Pam Grier never had. Instead, Grier worked for Samuel Z. Arkoff at American International Pictures and Roger Corman at New World Pictures, both of them masters of getting it done fast and getting it done cheap.

The movies Grier made at the height of her fame, from roughly 1971 to 1975, are the sort of tossed-together B vehicles usually populated by a disposable passel of starlets. Even the best of Grier's movies, *Coffy* (1973) and *Foxy Brown* (1974), both written and directed by Jack Hill, are cheap-looking, with dialogue and plots that are—barely—by the numbers, and acting that to call it broad would be to suggest nuance it doesn't have. The movies work because Hill, an old exploitation hand, had a sure sense of pacing and a knack for violent action scenes, and because—recognizing the commanding presence of his star—he allowed the camera and the audience to revel in her.

Thelma Ritter's famous response in *All About Eve* to Anne

Baxter's tale of woe—"Everything but the bloodhounds snappin' at her rear end"—might be Pam Grier's motto. Grier spends much of *Coffy* and *Foxy Brown* getting beaten, shot up with heroin, abducted, raped. She spends the rest of these pictures dishing out even worse revenge.

In the opening of *Coffy*, Grier pretends to be a strung-out party girl in order to lure a kingpin drug dealer to a private rendez-vous. Once there, she produces a sawed-off shotgun and announces, "This is the end of your rotten life, *you motherfuckin' dope pusher!*" And Hill thoughtfully positions the camera behind the baddie's Afro so we can watch his head blow apart as Grier pulls the trigger. It's one of those movie moments so abrupt and sadistic that you can't help but laugh, even as your jaw is doing a paratrooper drop into your lap. *Foxy Brown* ends with Grier confronting Ms. Big, the leader of a drug ring she funds through a top-of-the-line escort service, and presenting the woman with her lover's penis floating in a pickle jar. That's after Foxy has escaped from the desert shack where two rednecks have been shooting her up and then climbing on top of her. (One of them ends up with his eye gouged out by a clothes hanger before Grier douses him and his partner in gasoline and sets them on fire.)

Grier never condescends to these movies, or to the consider-ably shabbier ones that preceded them, like *Women in Cages* or Hill's good-natured and even less reputable *Big Doll House* (both entries in the once hugely popular women's-prison genre). Despite the abuse she takes and deals out, her dignity as a performer is never threatened, even during the copious and gratuitous nudity that was mandated to lure in the audience. Disrobing for a pimp in *Coffy*, Grier wears a sly, dirty smile that injects a conscious element of performance: She's nude but not naked. In some ways the truest love scenes Grier plays are the ones when she's delivering high kicks and karate chops, or using a sharpened bobby pin stashed in her Afro to stab the thug who means to have his way with her before dispatching her with an overdose of heroin. Grier brings much more passion to these moments than she does to the lovemaking scenes in which she's saddled with a procession of cloddish men. She's undeniably a star, but in a way that's a series of contradictions.

One of the paradoxes of the movies is that you can be a star—by which I mean you can display all the charisma and commanding presence and style that marks you as born to be in front of a camera—and never break out of second-rate movies or get the roles that you deserve. Conversely, it's possible to get those great roles and achieve huge success without ever possessing a star presence. Michelle Pfeiffer was a star from the moment she descended in that glass elevator in *Scarface*—although the automatic prejudice that assumes beautiful people can't act meant it took a while for people to see she was also an actress. Meryl Streep—always too busy being the straight-A student, nailing an accent the way the class grind nails a test—has never managed it. (Asked for her opinion of Streep's acting, Katharine Hepburn said, "Click, click, click.")

For all the pleasure there is in watching Pam Grier, despite her having become an icon revered in hip-hop culture—despite Quentin Tarantino, who with a fan's devotion and a director's masterstroke gave her the starring role in *Jackie Brown*—there's no escaping that she never had the career she should have. Pam Grier was a star, but only to black Americans. At the peak of her fame, if you had asked white American moviegoers to identify her, it's likely that even the ones who could have wouldn't have seen any movie she was in. She appeared on the cover of *Ms.*, but can you imagine anyone on that subscriber list going to see one of her movies?

Grier worked in blaxploitation movies, that genre that flour-
ished in roughly the same years she did, 1971 to '75, and featured
black heroes (often the same characters who would have been
villains in movies geared towards a white audience), urban settings,
R & B soundtracks, and plenty of violence. The theme songs for
the genre's biggest hits—Isaac Hayes's "Theme from 'Shaft'" and
"Superfly" (scored by Curtis Mayfield as a rebuke to that movie's
glorification of the pusher hero)—were all over AM radio. I can
remember hearing Mayfield's "Superfly" on the car radio as my
Dad and I left our local mall, but neither *Superfly* nor any other
blaxploitation picture would be playing at the mall's two-screen
theater.

Blaxploitation movies stayed in the city, and even there only at
certain theaters. And while some dedicated white moviegoers, or
hipsters out for an evening of cinematic slumming, might be among
the audiences, middle-class white moviegoers who wouldn't have
thought twice about going to see *The French Connection* or the
latest Clint Eastwood picture stayed away. For that matter, so did
middle-class black moviegoers. In a reflection of the second-rate
housing offered to black Americans in the aftermath of white flight,
the theaters that played the new black movies were often former
movie palaces that had been allowed to disintegrate.

In a remarkable passage in her wonderful *Third Girl from the
Left*, the novelist Martha Southgate captures the exhilaration and
bad aftertaste of blaxploitation's moment in movie culture:

> In 1971, Melvin Van Peebles made *Sweet Sweetback's Baadasssss
> Song* for $500,000. It earned $14 million. That's how it started.
> Both major studios and small, scruffy independents like Samuel
> Z. Arkoff's American International Pictures started turning out

cheaply made, bodacious, and hyperreal action pictures, starring black people, if not made by them, as fast as they could buy film stock. The most compelling of them, like *Sweetback*, with its mix of black power and misogyny, the thrill of watching a black man beat a cop to death with his own handcuffs (even though it took place out of camera range because it was just too expensive to make it look convincing), offered an evening of the score to those for whom the score had been so uneven for so very long. It was 1971, 1972, 1973. Martin Luther King, Jr., had been dead for four years, five years, six years, and peace had been given more than a chance. So to rise up in the theater, to look up in the theater and see yourself, no matter how manipulated and filmed and badly lit, and speaking crappy, unconvincing dialogue, to see yourself, to see your rage there for a minute—that was enough for a lot of folks. But then of course it all started to fall apart, almost the second it began. The flesh turned on the flesh. The NAACP called it out. The white people made all the money. The black actors got only dope and coke and cold fried chicken and pay that was less, far less, than union scale. And whatever the point had been got lost in a sea of Afro'd gun-totin' tough guys declaring war on the pushers and gettin' all the honeys. The honeys, as usual, had little to say. They got raped, they stood by their men, sometimes they stood up for themselves, but not without making their way through at least two to three nude scenes. The good times couldn't last forever. They never do . . .

The bone-deep weariness of those last two lines can't help but get to anyone who knows the old story Southgate is alluding to. It was a story that stretched back to performers like Ethel Waters and Pearl Bailey never really getting a chance to make their mark in movies. It encompassed Lena Horne, an obvious star, being denied the musical comedy roles she was made for. It took in Dorothy Dandridge, perhaps the best chance there had been for a black leading lady, not getting a role for four years after playing the lead in the 1954 film *Carmen Jones*, and dying at forty-two with $2.14 in her checking account. It took in the fiercely talented Diana Sands, who played Shakespeare and Shaw onstage but, before her early death from cancer, got only occasional movie or TV guest-star work. By the time Pam Grier was making movies, something like this was already playing out with Cicely Tyson, who, after the one-two punch of *Sounder* and *The Autobiography of Miss Jane Pittman*—performances that would have made a white actress immediately sought after—had only drab, mediocre film roles come her way. It would continue after Grier with the misuse—or nonuse—of actresses like Lonette McKee, Angela Bassett, Regina King. And it continues today with actresses as talented as Kerry Washington, Viola Davis, and Octavia Spencer turning to television because there are no leading roles for them in the movies.

The example that haunts me is Sharon Warren, who made an astonishing debut as Ray Charles's mother in the 2004 *Ray* and has gotten exactly one film role since.

In some ways the movie that might have changed all this, the 1972 Billie Holiday biopic *Lady Sings the Blues* starring Diana Ross, was also the movie that knew in its bones things weren't going to get better anytime soon. *Lady Sings the Blues* is a soapy, almost wholly fictional, and immensely entertaining treatment of the great jazz singer's life. Ross, swathed in a succession of satiny Bob Mackie gowns and so skinny she appeared to be all eyes and ruffles, gave black audiences the opportunity to bask in the kind of movie-star glamour white audiences had long taken for granted.

Ross provided the missing image that Gayle Pemberton wrote about in her searching essay "Do He Have Your Number, Mr. Jeffrey?" Pemberton, writing as a black American who loves the golden age of Hollywood movies, captures how it feels to be enraptured with something that, sooner or later, is bound to break your heart. Pemberton's mother was, as her daughter would be, one of the black movie fans who loved the same Hollywood movies that often showed stereotyped images of people who looked like them. Pemberton's mom was old enough to have seen the golden-age movies as they were released, instead of years later on TV, as her daughter often did. "Mother's was the perfect generation to see Hollywood movies when they were fresh, new, and perhaps more palpable than they are now," Pemberton writes, "when young French maids and their mothers, along with the impoverished, the disillusioned, the lost, and even the comfortable and secure, could sit before the silver screen and see a different world projected than the one they lived in. And they could dream."

Pemberton talks about the images of blacks that populated movies, dubious ones in big pictures, like Hattie McDaniel's Mammy in *Gone With the Wind*, who fulfills the stereotype of the bustling, irascible black mammy but is also, consistently, the most levelheaded character in the movie, one whose volubility and sheer size make her anything but subservient to the foolishness of her white masters. And also the characters in the movie equivalent of the chitlin circuit, the cheap B pictures made with black casts for black audiences. Pemberton writes of how her mother, having seen what Hollywood glamour could be, wasn't about to be fobbed off with these cheap imitations. She also writes about how the harshness of the lives that faced black moviegoers made them less susceptible to the romanticism of the movies—although it's a safe bet that poor white people in the Depression knew just how much of a fantasy they were seeing as well. So imagine you've watched stereotypes for years. Then you got to witness the emergence of performers who escaped those stereotypes, women like Lena Horne and Dorothy Dandridge, only to see them not getting leading roles. You settle into your seat in anticipation of Diana Ross—already a star by the time Hollywood approached her—on the big screen, embodying all the glamour the movies had never showcased in a black actress.

And then imagine Ross taking it all away.

To watch the opening shot of Diana Ross as Holiday, bound in a straitjacket, her wild hair and the gauntness of her face turning it into some awful Kabuki mask as she writhed in a padded cell, was to feel the cold point of a hypodermic being drawn down your spine. Ross's performance is alternately heartbreaking and terrifying, making us fall in love with this scrawny girl and then making us watch as heroin turns her fresh, untutored eagerness into a slurred, sleepy doper's cool. The picture went on as a triumph-and-tears star turn of the Susan Hayward variety, while Ross went another way, raw and unprotected and frighteningly deliberate. Ross the singer couldn't replicate the cold, hard edge you sometimes hear in Holiday's voice, so she put it into the performance, reminding the audience of the self-destruction and the festering wounds that went into that voice of romantic defeat so many of us have wallowed in. Billie Holiday is the sound of our romantic dreams. Diana Ross set out to steal our sleep. It was hard to watch, and a white viewer could only imagine how much harder for a black audience. If this was the glamour that movies gave black audiences, they were going to have to pay for every bit of pleasure. And if you have to pay even for pleasure, why not strike out to keep yourself from being a victim?

Ross's performance was of a piece with the black music that was on the radio at the time—music that, as Greil Marcus laid out in the haunted essay on Sly Stone in his book *Mystery Train: Images of America in Rock 'n' Roll Music*, was rooted in the implosion of the hope and unity of the civil rights years, and the separatism and bitterness that defined life for black Americans under Nixon. None stronger than Sly and the Family Stone's *There's a Riot Goin' On*, a sinister, insinuating, insular album that turned its back on the inclusiveness and good vibes that had made the band so popular with white and black audiences.

"Almost always," Marcus writes, "there is a retreat once something like the truth is out. Audiences respond to that moment of clarity, but they only want so much of it." Blaxploitation is part of that retreat. *Riot* and the other black music Marcus writes about were about how the role of the hustler, adopted as a rejection of black subservience, became its own trap. Blaxploitation was the hustler glorified. "In uptown movie houses across the country," Marcus wrote, "Staggerlee killed and fucked and killed and fucked and the white sheriff near died of envy and Billy died to let Stack kill and fuck another day."

At the time, there were two schools of thought on blaxploitation. There were the aisle-seat revolutionaries who turned up amid the film critics of the day, ready to hail the new movies as authentic images of blacks standing up to the corruption and degradation of white-dominated society (specifically and usually the Italian gangsters in league with the cops and politicians). And there was the more prevalent disapproval of high-minded critics—almost all of them white—which held that blaxploitation movies were crass and violent outings financed by white movie executives getting rich by exploiting the fears of the black audience. It's important to note, though, that the motivation for making blaxploitation pictures was the same as the motivation for making almost anything else: money. And when MGM was saved from bankruptcy by the surprise success of *Shaft,* there was even more incentive to keep making them. "[Dr. King's] dream has been Shafted, Hammered, Slaughtered," wrote Pauline Kael, invoking the names of three of the biggest blaxploitation hits. She wasn't wrong. The new black movies—which were, after all, exploitation movies—didn't work on the most honorable instincts of their target audience. At their ugliest, as Kael knew, the movies were selling the idea of blacks as permanent victims and any hope of escaping oppression through education or hard work or legislation as a white man's con.

Still, the line isn't one of Kael's finest moments. It's hardly disavowing King's rigorous philosophy of nonviolence to say that by 1972, when those lines were written, the triumphs of the civil rights years seemed very far away. To the white liberals who had been allies in those years, it was a battle they imagined had already been mostly won. It wasn't the black movies that were destroying King's dream, it was the aftermath of the "benign neglect" of the Nixon years. It was how that neglect made it easy for white people—even some who should have known better—to believe—even if they didn't say it out loud—that after all the time and money and government programs spent on black Americans, it must be their own fault if they hadn't improved their lot.

And the line is also an uncharacteristic slide into the sort of moralism Kael usually disdained. In her great essay "Trash, Art and the Movies," Kael said of the pleasures of movie violence, "Because we feel low we sink in the boredom, relax in the irresponsibility, and maybe grin for a minute when the gunman lines up three men and kills them with a single bullet, which is no more 'real' to us than the nursery-school story of the brave little tailor." Black audiences went to the action movies aimed at them just as white audiences went to see Clint Eastwood or Charles Bronson. They went to escape responsibility for a few hours and enjoy the fantasy of solving the scariest problems of the world by kicking ass. Kael had to know that nobody went to an action movie to emulate Dr. King. You don't go to see a picture called *Boss Nigger* to be uplifted. You go because it's low-down and funny and because there's a kick in seeing Fred Williamson as a black bounty hunter who appoints himself sheriff of a small town and scares Whitey to death. Black moviegoers should have been able to enjoy the revenge fantasies that action movies specialize in without being treated as if they were failing a civics exam. As Greil Marcus wrote about the black audience for these movies: "That audience had a right to revenge." And if, as Kael writes, being in those audiences could be an uncomfortable experience for white moviegoers, she also knew, as she wrote in her review of *The Warriors*—a movie that got the panties of the nation's moral watchdogs in a collective twist—"If there's one immutable law about movies, it may be that middle-class people get all hot and bothered whenever there's a movie that the underclass really responds to."

And then there was the pleasure for black audiences of getting to see black faces on the screen. If none came near Grier's charisma or, as her later career would reveal, her depth, there was still the pleasure to be had in drinking in the good looks and charm of the likes of Fred Williamson, Tamara Dobson, and Richard Roundtree. There was, just as there had been in '30s movies, character actors who essayed immediately recognizable types. D'Urville Martin was always fast-talking his way out of a tight spot; Antonio Fargas was all twitchy trouble; Sid Haig always seemed to be enjoying the unfolding of some sly private joke.

Of course, blaxploitation's fantasies didn't offer anything like an accounting of how, during the civil rights years, black Americans lived out a daily demonstration of the cost—and the worth—of citizenship. They were still living it out even as the civil rights movement splintered and drugs flooded black neighborhoods. (It took until 2010 and Tanya Hamilton's extraordinary film *Night Catches Us*, the story of two former Black Panthers in mid-'70s Philadelphia, for American movies to tell the story of people who had fought for black rights carrying on in a decade in which the struggle was regarded as already won.) Blaxploitation movies were, implicitly and explicitly, a rejection of the higher ethos of the civil rights years.

There's something undeniably ugly in exploitation movies telling people, intentionally or not, that the changes they've worked for and sacrificed for have been a sucker's bargain—that, by following the rules, they've been Whitey's dupes once again. It's a given in these films that black people can't rely on the cops, who are always in bed with the mob, readily doling out protection to the crooks in return for a cut of the action. The movies appear to be delivering the message that black people have the power to take their lives into their own hands. But it's hard to credit them with that when they play on feelings of black helplessness and despair. The hillbillies who keep Grier captive in *Foxy Brown* lasso her with a rope when she tries to escape, a moment meant to call up images of black people being lynched and black women being raped by their slave masters. But my God is it fun when Grier unleashes her revenge.

Like the gangsta images of hip-hop, blaxploitation offered a disreputable form of feel-good minstrelsy. Despite the occasional attempts to confuse the pleasure we take in the revenge these movies dish out with revolutionary statements; despite the lapses into ugliness (like the moment in *Shaft* when the dirty cop is pointedly called "Lebowitz," the emphasis on his Jewishness); despite the brutality in movies not nearly so much fun as *Coffy* and *Foxy Brown*, there's no denying that blaxploitation allowed many black moviegoers their first images of black heroes, affording them some of the good, disreputable pleasures that white audiences had enjoyed for years at shoot-'em-ups and gangster films.

Blaxploitation took the macho stance of the black-power movement, the Stagger-Lee-as-revolutionary poses of Eldridge Cleaver and Huey Newton and H. Rap Brown and melded them to the most simplistic and rabble-rousing aspects of the vigilante movies of the era, like *Dirty Harry* and *Death Wish*. It would be too much to make a feminist claim for *Coffy* and *Foxy Brown*. And not because Grier isn't a strong, independent woman in them (in her memoir, *Foxy: My Life in Three Acts*, written with Andrea Cagan, Grier says that she modeled Coffy on her mother, who was also a nurse, and Foxy on her quick-tempered aunt Mennon) but because the movies are too steeped in exploitation staples. The girls get naked whenever they can, even if it's just lounging around a hotel suite waiting for the next assignment from their madam. And, in *Coffy*, Hill can't resist staging a food-fueled catfight between Coffy, posing as a Jamaican call girl, and the pimp's main squeeze, a skinny, jealous blonde. That character is pretty much par for the way white women appear in these movies: hookers who suck up to black pimps and pushers for the perks their money can give them, or *Foxy Brown*'s madam/drug kingpin, or the inhabitants of a lesbian bar depicted in a way that makes the Teamsters look like the Rockettes. If hit men turn up to kill a black pusher while he's in bed with his white woman, we have to see her breasts before she's killed along with him.

And both *Coffy* and *Foxy Brown* flirt with a kind of genre passing, the sporadic attempt to portray the move to run dope dealers and corrupt cops out of black neighborhoods, as if these were dramas of black self-determination instead of vigilante movies. Sometimes they try to do both at once. Whenever Jack Hill's script strands Grier with a speech about how the cops and politicians are in the pocket of the gangsters and there's nothing left for honest people to do except play as dirty as the dealers who've flooded black neighborhoods with drugs, you're right back listening to the windiest rationalizations of *Dirty Harry*'s advocation of barbarism. The speeches stick out because elsewhere Hill, wily enough to know what his audiences want, doesn't waste time justifying the violent solutions employed by his heroine and her allies. At its lightest it's a kind of slapstick vigilantism, as in *Foxy Brown* when a group of black revolutionaries who've formed what they call "the anti-slavery com-mitt-tee" disguise themselves as winos and bums in order to bust the street dealers openly operating in their neighborhood. The sequence delivers the almost childish pleasure of watching the bad guys take a whupping. The dealers aren't turned over to the cops (who are likely on the dealers' pad anyway) but taken for a ride (to a train heading out of town, we're told, but really, no one would complain if it were to a convenient dumping site). It's like the moment in the precode melodrama *Night Nurse* when Barbara Stanwyck's bootlegger boyfriend casually arranges to have the hood chauffeur who's roughed up Stanwyck bumped off. *Foxy Brown* has an even better bit: a drug kingpin hightailing it out of a tough spot finds that the crooked cops he's placed on patrol have been replaced by those same black vigilantes, now in the uniforms of the cops they've disarmed and stashed away.

You can't, however, make the same claim of innocent pleasure at the end of the movie when those vigilantes capture the kingpin and cut off his penis (the one that ends up in the pickle jar). These are not innocent movies, and their heroes and heroines have moved well beyond the reluctance to kill, the respect for violence—by which I mean the knowledge of what it is, the refusal either to glorify or pretend that it is unknown—that the critic Robert Warshow elucidated in his essay "Movie Chronicle: The Westerner." Describing the Western hero as "a figure of repose," Warshow wrote that he cannot communicate to others the pointlessness of being against killing or being killed. "There is no point being 'against' these things: they belong to his world," Warshow wrote. The vigilante movies had already moved beyond that acceptance, into the hero's refusal to feel regret for the choices forced upon him, or to believe that their enemies might feel pain.

Coffy and Foxy Brown are both out for revenge, Coffy on the dealers who hooked her eleven-year-old sister on heroin, Foxy on the dealers who killed her lover, an undercover cop working to bring them down. And from the moment she blasts that dope pusher's head apart in *Coffy* to the moment she shows the villainess what she's done to her lover in *Foxy Brown*, Pam Grier doesn't waste a moment of regret. None of the villains are given enough dimension to make you believe that killing them constitutes killing a human being. These are not, as *Superfly* was, movies on the side of the hustler. As Grier plays the characters, it's impossible to think of either Coffy or Foxy Brown as being vessels for the cunningly displaced macho attitudes of the movies with the black superstud heroes.

The confidence of Grier's heroines doesn't preclude them from showing fear. She's not an inhuman revenge machine. On the contrary, bruised and sweating and giving rein to the electric current of anger just below her skin, she's a palpably *human* revenge machine. During the most horrific acts she's called on to perform—holding a sawed-off rifle on a dealer as she forces him to inject a hot shot, going after a redneck's eye with a hook improvised from wire hangers—there's an element of disgust mingled with rage that gives Grier's actions a jolt beyond standard exploitation-movie excess.

In the less fraught scenes, Grier brings to her roles a strong element of play. When she and Robert Doqui play call girl and pimp in a scene from *Coffy*, they're like two kids showing off their bravado at a slightly naughty masquerade ball. James George's witty costuming abets them. Doqui has an outrageous canary-yellow cape-and-jumpsuit combo, and Grier, in some impossibly slinky paneled shifts, has enough seashells draped around her neck and wrists to look as if she's raided Neptune's treasure chest. Grier is even better in the scene in *Foxy Brown* where she tries to convince a drug dealer's pilot (blaxploitation stalwart Sid Haig) to fly her to the moon, or at least to the border. Getting an eyeful of her sitting alone at a bar, Haig looks like a man who spies a winning lottery ticket sitting unattended. Letting his eyes drink in every centimeter, he instructs the barman, "Get this dusky young lady whatever it is she needs to quench her magnificent thirst." Later, as his passenger on a drug run, Grier is playing drunk and high and horny while he's trying to keep his mind on business, and the two have the loose rapport of born clowns who have stumbled onto each other's wavelength. Undercover as a hooker—again—in *Foxy Brown*, Grier is assigned to service a corrupt white judge and convince him to free two pushers who'll come before him the next day. Foxy and her cohort turn the scene into a vaudeville routine in which the two women get back at the old white lecher. They pull down his trousers to reveal a pair of boxers adorned with big red hearts. And when they pull those down, Grier conducts an extended commentary on what, lying before her, turns out to be not so extended. It's a bit of low comedy that has nothing to do with uplifting the race but much to do with the disreputable pleasure of the movies.

Maybe that's the problem for some people.

Part of the pleasure of watching Sidney Poitier as a black Sherlock Holmes in *In the Heat of the Night* was getting to see him be immodest for a change. Poitier had long been saddled playing role models instead of characters, stuck with parts in which he was expected to be a spokesman for black Americans instead of an actor. After years of seeing him have to be better than anyone else in the room—but humble, always humble—it was a kick to see him act openly superior to the dogged white southern sheriff (Rod Steiger) he was assisting in a murder investigation. It was a pleasure to get to see him be sly and witty. It was easy to understand the desire for the upright, dignified image Poitier had been asked to play. Dumb racist roles had stymied generations of black actors before Poitier. But Poitier was straitjacketed, too, by the collective good intentions of the Perfect Negro roles he was given and by the burden of being a representative of all African Americans. Poitier is one of the most charismatic and polished and sexy movie stars to emerge after World War II, and he only rarely got to exude star power. Denzel Washington has had an easier time of it (especially when he was working with the late Tony Scott, who, along with Carl Franklin, understood Washington's strengths and limitations better than any other director) and had a far greater variety of roles than Poitier ever got. Still, when he won an Oscar for his gleefully nasty performance as a crooked cop in *Training Day*, Washington had to listen to people claim that he should have been nominated for playing admirable characters in *Malcolm X* and *The Hurricane*, even though those were stiff Great Men performances that fit the stiffness of the movies they were in.

If there were any doubt that the expectation that black actors need to be role models had abated, Viola Davis and Octavia Spencer learned otherwise on February 9, 2012. It was a week before the Oscars. Davis and Spencer had both been nominated for playing maids in the film version of Kathryn Stockett's best seller *The Help*, and they were appearing on Tavis Smiley's PBS talk show. What ensued was a master class in what happens when public relations are assumed to be the same thing as art. After assuring his guests that he was there to "celebrate" their achievement, Smiley confessed to "an ambivalence" that seventy-three years after Hattie McDaniel won an Oscar for playing Mammy, black actresses were still getting nominated for playing maids. Spencer was polite but firm, pointing out that if it wasn't a problem for Anthony Hopkins and Charlize Theron to win Oscars for playing serial killers, there should be no problem for her or Davis being honored for playing earnest, hard-working women. These characters, she told Smiley later in the interview, were their mothers and grandmothers, and there was no shame in the work they did.

Davis wasn't having any of it. "Do I always have to be noble?" she asked Smiley, before going on: "That very mind-set that you have, and that a lot of African Americans have, is absolutely destroying the black artist." Smiley, trying to appear unruffled, sat there. But Davis wasn't done. "Black artists cannot live in a revisionist place," she said, "can only tell the truth about humanity, and humanity is messy, people are messy . . . We as African Americans are more concerned with image and message and not execution—which is why every time you see our images they've been watered down to a point where they are not realistic at all. All of our humanity has been washed out." The conversation moved on to the lack of good roles for black actors and the persistence of insulting stereotypes. But it seemed like an afterthought. Davis was arguing for black actors to be free from being role models. Smiley was stumping for what might be called Talented Tenth moviemaking.

There were things left unsaid. No one talked about the racism that white liberal audiences routinely accept, the most glaring recent example being *Precious*, a horror show of black dysfunction that might have been conceived as a dramatization of the Moynihan report. It was, as the late Albert Murray had said years before about another of those works, Claude Brown's *Manchild in the Promised Land*, "social science fiction." In response to the claim that Brown's book "reveals what it is really like to be a Negro," Murray wrote, "It does no such thing. It tells [readers] absolutely nothing about Willie the Lion Smith, Sugar Ray Robinson, Adam Clayton Powell, Constance Baker Motley, the chief of maintenance at Lenox Tower, the barman at Smalls Paradise, the society editor at the *Amsterdam News*."

But listening to Davis talk about the censure that awaits the black artist who thinks in terms of individuals and not role models, you had to think of what might be called the black folk artists, the ones whose work wasn't about delicacy or subtlety: people like the vaudevillian Pigmeat Markham (who cleaned up the act that delighted black audiences when it was deemed undignified) or the great stand-up comic Moms Mabley, or later Redd Foxx and Richard Pryor. And you had to think of Pam Grier, possessed of an elegance that made her a creature from a place very different from the one folk artists inhabit but whose characters and whose most popular vehicles embraced a low-down appeal. Grier was adored as a star by the audiences who saw her at the time, unknown to white audiences and languished for years after her blaxploitation heyday.

If *Coffy* and *Foxy Brown* are the movies that created Pam Grier the icon, it's others you have to turn to for Pam Grier the actress. She's terrifying in *Fort Apache, The Bronx* as a junkie-hooker with dead eyes who kills both for the sheer fun of it and as distractedly as if she were flicking away crumbs.

But it's *Jackie Brown* that haunts all of Grier's other films now. Intended as a paean to Grier, Quentin Tarantino's version of Elmore Leonard's novel *Rum Punch* (in which Grier's character is a blonde named Jackie Burke) is the finest role Grier ever played. Underrated when it appeared in 1997—by me, among other critics—the movie has now come to be thought of as something close to an American classic. It's as rich an examination of camaraderie, as well as a demonstration of action as character, as American movies have seen since Howard Hawks's *Rio Bravo*. It's another Hawks movie, though—1966's *El Dorado*, a dark romp shot through with a deep knowledge of the pain and dignity of aging—that *Jackie Brown* also recalls. The duets between Grier and Robert Forster, as the bail bondsman who springs her and then falls for her—hard—are all, essentially, love scenes, even when the two are just talking, just sitting in her apartment over coffee, listening to the Delfonics. American movies don't afford this level of longing and desire to people past their forties, and Grier and Forster represent a now-rare breed in American movies among characters of any age: people deeply comfortable with who they are.

And yet, for all that confidence, Tarantino allows Grier the uncertainty of an adult entering middle age, no longer sure she has the strength to start over, terrified of where she's headed. You look at the furniture in her small, spare apartment, at the collection of

LPs lovingly tended because she doesn't have the money to start her collection over with CDs, and you see something like the same furnishings in Foxy's apartment, twenty years later, moved from place to place over the years, taken care of because it's all she can afford, and you understand Jackie as the older, wiser version of those characters. Grier essays the role with incredible grace and goes beyond it, making the movie an elegy for a career that should have leapt beyond the tawdry confines of blaxploitation. That she hasn't had a role to equal *Jackie Brown* seems, while you are watching the movie, inexplicable. And then, after the magic of the movie lifts and you survey the landscape of roles for black middle-aged women, it makes all the sense in the world.

And it makes that part of our movie heritage seem shameful. You could invoke Gloria Swanson's line from *Sunset Boulevard*— "It's the pictures that got small"—to explain Pam Grier's career arc, but it wouldn't be quite right. It's likely that most movies would have been too small to contain the magnificence of Pam Grier. The crime is that they never even tried.

WHITE MAN'S BURDEN: *ULZANA'S RAID*

THERE WAS NO better way to have a lousy time at the movies in the late '60s and early '70s than to go see a Western. Grounded as they are in America's founding myth of pioneer expansionism, Westerns, during the Vietnam years, became a way to depict America as having always been a nation of racist thugs, ready to eliminate whatever people of color made us feel uncomfortable. The new anti-Westerns, as they were called, operated from the belief—mistaken—that until then the genre had primarily been oaters for morons ready to ignore the blood-stains on our patriotic myths and swallow a simpleminded moral scheme in which the white hats saved the town, or the settlers' farm, or the schoolmarm's virtue, from the black hats and the redskins.

You can't offer any higher praise to Robert Aldrich's 1972 Western *Ulzana's Raid* than to say that it seems designed to upset everyone's most reassuring political shibboleths. Ulzana is an Apache who leads a war party off the government agency where his people have been sequestered and on a rampage of murder, rape, and mutilation. McIntosh (Burt Lancaster), a veteran tracker, is sent out to capture Ulzana accompanied by a division of cavalry under the command of the green and untested Lieutenant DeBuin (Bruce Davison).

Even in a time of often brutal Westerns—movies that used the slaughter of Indians to whip audiences into an almost voluptuous frenzy of outrage—*Ulzana* is one grisly picture. Early on, a settler sends his wife and young son away from their farm while he stays behind to guard it. The woman and boy are in the company of a scout meant to lead them to the safety of the cavalry fort. In the midst of their journey, Apaches on horseback appear on a far ridge and begin galloping towards them. The scout digs his spurs into his horse's flanks and takes off. The woman stands in her wagon screaming at the scout not to leave her. As if recalled to duty, the scout halts his horse, turns it around, and gallops back towards her. The woman clasps her hands and looks heavenward, giving thanks, her face torn between terror and the rapture of someone for whom deliverance is nigh. And deliverance comes, seconds later, when the scout puts a bullet through her forehead. That bright red hole appears like the punch line to a joke that's been told too fast for us to grasp. We feel the shock of it, but the *why*—that this death is more merciful than what would have awaited her at the hands of the Apaches—takes a second to sink in. And still the scene doesn't relent. The scout grabs the boy from beside his mother's corpse, plunks him on his horse and tries to make a getaway. The Apaches shoot the horse out from under the scout, sending both him and the boy tumbling to the ground. The scout seizes his pistol, jams it in his mouth and blows off the back of his head. The boy, alone now, runs to the buckboard, where the Apaches are already rifling through the family belongings, one kneeling near his mother's corpse, about to take a knife to sever her dead fingers when he can't pry off her wedding ring. The boy shoos him away, works the ring off, and gives it to the Apache. In the distance, three Apaches who have been kneeling over the scout's corpse suddenly stand back from it, laughing as they toss the dead man's heart back and forth.

We are very far here from the traditional Westerns that allowed us to cheer guiltlessly for the cavalry. We are also far from the counterculture view of American military force as the vanguard of genocide, and of Indians as peaceful people who want only to live off the land according to their traditions. (Liberal audiences, missing the condescension, had found that an especially comforting view.)

Of course, those traditional Westerns never were as simple or rah-rah American as they were treated. Not just the tough, downbeat, morally conflicted '50s Westerns from directors like Budd Boetticher, Anthony Mann, Delmer Daves, and Aldrich himself, but often the Westerns that preceded them: classics like *Red River*, *My Darling Clementine*, and *Stagecoach*. America, in *Stagecoach*— the idea of America, the freedom from judgment, the freedom to be—always exists somewhere else, a place the country reaches for and will never realize.

"It is just the march of civilization that forces the Westerner to move on . . ." the critic Robert Warshow wrote about twelve years after *Stagecoach*. Arguing for the moral rectitude of the Western hero and for the austerity of the form, Warshow said, "The Westerner imposes himself by the appearance of unshakable control . . . It is a crucial point of honor *not* to 'do it first'; his gun remains in its holster until the moment of combat . . . The Westerner is the last gentleman, and the movies which over and over again tell his story are probably the last art form in which the concept of honor retains its strength."

Honor was nowhere to be found in the '60s and '70s anti-Westerns that Warshow would not live to see. You could sum up the entire genre variant by calling it "Phnom on the Range." The lone, patient Westerner, slow to violence and loath to either glory in it or apologize when he did resort to it, became the racist gunslinger (or soldier) ready to bring the scourge of the White Man down on those who would stand in his way.

Reviewing Abraham Polonsky's 1969 *Tell Them Willie Boy Is Here*, Pauline Kael wrote, "If Americans have always been as ugly and brutal and hypocritical as some of our current movies keep telling us, there's nothing for us to do but commit genosuicide."

Pictures like *Willie Boy* and *Soldier Blue* seized on Vietnam to turn the genre into portraits of the inbred, genocidal murderousness of white Americans. You knew before you settled into your seat that it was only a matter of time before some Native people would start to have their innards smeared over those vast landscapes that years of going to Westerns had taught us to enjoy.

Of all the bad times to be had, none was worse than Arthur Penn's 1970 adaptation of Thomas Berger's Western picaresque *Little Big Man*. Starting out as a tall tale with Dustin Hoffman as a naïf who wanders the Old West, the movie provides a reasonably engaging hour of comic absurdity until you realize you're meant to pay for every laugh the movie has given you until then, and the slaughters and bromides ("The white man . . . believes everything is dead") start piling up. It was particularly depressing coming from Arthur Penn, who, in the films that preceded *Little Big Man*—the Depression-set *Bonnie and Clyde* and *Alice's Restaurant*, his melancholy elegy for the counterculture in which '60s hippies were presented as the shaggy descendants of the American transcendentalists—had refused to allow either the characters or the audience to feel superior to the America that was onscreen. In *Little Big Man*, Penn offered audiences the kind of self-loathing that is actually a path to superiority. Moviegoers could engage in collective breast-beating over the stain of genocide on our national identity, all the while separating themselves from that identity.

When it comes to educated, liberal American audiences, that kind of self-loathing is usually a safe bet. It was during Vietnam when Susan Sontag interrupted her devotions at the altar of white European culture to deliver herself of the opinion that "the white race is the cancer of human history." And it was right after 9/11 when Sontag, who had spent the forty-eight hours following the attacks monitoring the events in New York and Washington via the television in her Berlin hotel room, informed us that they were "undertaken as a consequence of specific American alliances and actions." This, even though no one had claimed responsibility. The belief that we are essentially racist killers—of Indians or Vietnamese or Muslims—has always been too tempting for many Americans to resist.

The basic appeal is the ease of substituting ideology—any ideology, which always makes the conversation stupider—for the inconvenient facts and hard choices and unclean pragmatism with which history and politics present us. But there's also the great pleasure of exempting yourself from your history, and being able to say that whatever sins were done in the name of your country have nothing to do with you. In this view, wiping out the Indians, or lynching black southerners, or torturing Iraqis, becomes not a debasement of America but its fulfillment as the world's foremost exporter of war and genocide. Talk to Americans who believe that and it's hard not to come to the conclusion that, on some level, they regard themselves as having been born here by mistake, placed among barbarians and dolts when they are clearly made of much more refined stuff.

Given the era in which *Ulzana's Raid* was produced—a time when, in good movies and bad, audiences didn't expect things to turn out for the better—it's no surprise that few of either Ulzana's raiding party or the trackers survive, and that the horrors along the way just keep on coming. It's a determinedly grim movie. In one sequence, the homesteader who sends his family away is found tied to a post, scalped and disemboweled, his dog's severed tail stuffed in his mouth. "Why would they do that?" asks DeBuin, only to have McIntosh answer, "Apaches have a strange sense of humor." Not only is the young lieutenant denied an explanation that makes sense to him, he's told that this horror is meant as a joke. The gulf revealed in that exchange—not just the gulf between the white man and the Apache but the gulf between the white man who can't fathom irrationality and the one who accepts it as the way things are—can stand for the entire movie. Over the 103 minutes of *Ulzana's Raid*, no explanations will be forthcoming.

There's never a moment in which Aldrich or screenwriter Alan Sharp deny the ugly legacy of what was done to the Indians: the stolen land, the massacres, the broken treaties, the sequestration on government "agencies." But they ask us to hold in our heads the possibility that Apaches could be both victimized and brutal. And they go further by suggesting that this incomprehensible brutality is not solely a reaction to American persecution.

In one scene DeBuin tries to get Ke-Ni-Tay (Jorge Luke), the Apache tracker who works with the cavalry, to make sense of what he's witnessing. DeBuin, the son of an eastern minister who only a few days into his trek has already seen more savagery than anything in his good Christian upbringing could ever have led him to imagine—more than anyone should ever be expected to see— wants to know how the Apaches can be so brutal. He wants to know, for instance, why a raiding party spared the life of the settler's son, found beside his dead mother. Sharp—in a perfect example of how his screenplays could be both intelligent and impossibly literary at the same time—gives Ke-Ni-Tay a speech in which he answers DeBuin that Ulzana and his party are killing "to take the power. Each man that die, the man who kill him take his power. Man give up his power when he die. Like fire with heat. Fire that burn long time. Many can have heat . . . Here in this land man must have power." Get over the thesis statements of those lines and you're still left with a logic that provides no comfort. The little boy wasn't spared out of any sense of mercy but because a little boy has no power worth possessing. Later, when the regiment finds a woman who has been raped into a state of madness—a woman who would ordinarily have been killed by the Apaches—they are told that the reason she's been left alive is to saddle the cavalry with her care, thus diminishing *their* power.

Sharp (who died in 2013), as well as the movie's admirers, inevitably spoke of *Ulzana's Raid* as a metaphor for Vietnam. And at times that's the parallel he's pushing, the notion that the white man has driven the Native warrior to this level of savagery, as when he has Ke-Ni-Tay explain, "Ulzana is long time in the agency. His power very thin. Smell in his nose is old smell of the agency. Old smell. Smell of woman, smell of dog, smell of children. Man with old smell in the nose is old man. Ulzana came loose for new smell. Pony running, the smell of burning, the smell of bullet—for power!" But explanation does not equal justification. The horrors of the movie are so vividly imagined that no explanation can diminish the fact of them, just as the psychiatrist's explanation at the finish of *Psycho* dissolves into meaninglessness in the face of Norman Bates's insane grin.

Aldrich is up to something much less morally neat than Sharp. He could be a crude, abrasive director, and *Ulzana's Raid* doesn't escape an element of rubbing our noses in the savagery. But for all the movie's shock and perhaps because of the abruptness of the horrors, it's characterized by matter-of-factness, by the physical specificity of the direction. Most of *Ulzana's Raid* was shot in the Arizona desert in bright daylight. We see everything with an almost stark clarity: the men on horseback; McIntosh, the grizzled scout, in his well-worn buckskins; the lines of cavalry in their trim navy-blue uniforms; the hills and dusty vistas. We see the familiar sights Westerns have accustomed us to, much of it bathed in the peculiarly distinct frontier light that calls up the paintings of Frederic Remington: light that looks less as if it were emanating from a single source than from a million different particles scattered throughout the air. The harshness of the movie is that Aldrich and his director of photography, Joseph Biroc, present the savagery with the same clarity, even when we see only its aftermath. That's especially true given Biroc's uncluttered compositions. There's none of the Hieronymus-Bosch-meets-Manifest-Destiny phoniness that characterizes the aestheticized pulp of Cormac McCarthy's novel *Blood Meridian*. The sequence with the mercy killing of the woman and the scout's subsequent suicide is so awful because every action that seems cowardly or brutal—the Scout's impulse to flee; his killing of the woman; his own suicide; the woman's plea not to be left alone and her thankfulness for her impending murder; the boy's shockingly intimate contact with his dead mother as he places her finger in his mouth to loosen her wedding ring—has behind it the aim of avoiding something far worse.

What can't be given a rational explanation is the brutality of the Indians. Ke-Ni-Tay's speech about how Ulzana needs to take power from his victims makes sense when we hear it. It's reinforced by the way the defeated look on Ke-Ni-Tay's face—the look of someone who realizes he's caught between betraying his people and staying with them as they are wiped out—gives way to a fleeting vitality as he describes the power Ulzana seeks. But even in that speech Ke-Ni-Tay speaks of Ulzana's dedication to carnage not as revenge but as simply the way his people are. Which is precisely the gulf Aldrich and Sharp force us to confront. You can find a logic in killing a member of the race who decimated your people. But even those who approve of that Old Testament justice might be hard-pressed to pretend to understand what Aldrich shows us in the aftermath of the act: Ulzana's raiding party using their victim's heart in a game of catch.

The key exchange of the movie comes on that rancher's farm after his body has been buried, the ghastliness of what transpired now hidden but not forgotten. It's nighttime. The men are finishing their supper, talking, getting into their bedrolls, dreading the next day on the trail when God knows what else they'll find. McIntosh, apparently undisturbed, is preparing to sleep in the dead man's bed, when he's approached by DeBuin, still shaken by what he's found. The young lieutenant asks him, "Do you hate Apaches, Mr. McIntosh?" No, McIntosh says, and DeBuin replies, "I do." "Well," McIntosh says, "it might not make you happy, Lieutenant, but it sure won't make you lonesome." There's more than a trace of condescension in McIntosh's answer. Lancaster's blindingly white smile could convey great warmth or the single-minded ruth-lessness of a shark closing in for the kill. He had a way of using his rolling, enunciated delivery as a vehicle of sharp irony delivered via the disguise of false bonhomie. McIntosh has already heard, count-less times from countless people, all the arguments that DeBuin, the moral virgin, is going to make. He knows just how easy hating the Apaches is for DeBuin, for most white men. And he knows how, in DeBuin, that hatred is as untested as any of this boy offi-cer's other cherished principles. DeBuin persists. Why doesn't McIntosh hate the Apaches? he wants to know. This time there's no condescension in McIntosh's answer, just truth the young man is not ready to comprehend. "It would," says McIntosh, "be like hating the desert because there's no water in it."

And that's the movie in thirteen words. There's a weird level of respect in McIntosh's line. Not for DeBuin, who expects the world to share the values of white Christian men—values that even DeBuin himself is ready to abandon when, for instance, he orders Ke-Ni-Tay to be the one to bury the bodies of Ulzana's victims. Even a seeming act of decency on DeBuin's part—ordering his men not to mutilate an Apache corpse—is presented as a bit of moral arrogance. It's typical of how the movie complicates our responses that it chooses to see DeBuin's preventing an atrocity as part of his naïve willingness to divide the world into Christians and heathens. He doesn't care that Apache corpses might be mutilated. McIntosh calls him on the real source of his outrage when he says, "What bothers you, Lieutenant, is you don't like to think of white men behaving like Indians. It kind of confuses the issue, don't it?"

The integrity of *Ulzana's Raid* is that it doesn't pretend—whether in our nobler aspects or our baser ones—that we are all brothers under the skin. What makes *Ulzana's Raid* so potentially troubling for good liberal humanist moviegoers is that, via DeBuin's Christianity, it shows them a reflection of their own progressive rationalism, depicted as inadequate to deal with the reality of the horror they are watching.

If there is a deep and understandable human desire to turn to the *why*, there is, in the liberal-rational mind, an equally deep expectation that a reason can always be found. "There is nothing worse," writes the English academic Katharine Angel in her book *Unmastered*, "for middle-class intellectuals, raised in secular rationalism and its own peculiar fundamentalism, than being irrational." To insist there is a rational explanation to irrational acts—an insistence epitomized by Sontag's "specific American alliances and actions"—is to diminish the very horror of those events.

For some progressives, insisting on the irrationality of certain atrocities is tantamount to turning your back on centuries of Enlightenment thought, becoming the equivalent of the bigots who throw up their hands and proclaim, "What do you expect of those people? They're crazy."

Ulzana's Raid makes accepting the irrational especially hard for liberal moviegoers by embodying the irrational in a people who were themselves victims. For many people, victimization, especially at the hands of America, trumps all else. In the year *Ulzana's Raid* was released, Joan Baez was part of a group that traveled to Hanoi and spent a month living under an American bombing raid, an action that further solidified her heroism among the left. Seven years later, Baez was at the forefront of a group of people who placed a full-page ad in the *Washington Post* writing of the "nightmare" that the triumphant Communist regime had made of life in Vietnam, jailing and disappearing those perceived to be political enemies. Suddenly, Baez was no longer a hero but a propagandist for the mind-set that had brought us into the war in the first place, when what she had actually done was to demonstrate the ability to hold two contradictory facts in her head at the same time.

It's not surprising that there wasn't much of an appetite for *Ulzana's Raid*'s thorny insistence on refusing its audiences the comfort of their own moral impotence during the waning days of our involvement in Vietnam. Nobody likes to be made to feel that *their* moral outrage is too easy. There may be even less appetite for that now, what with the manner in which the Iraq War was used by some to retrospectively paint American grief and rage and confusion over 9/11 as typical Yankee egocentrism, America saying that its grief was the only one that mattered. In effect, that attitude accomplished the linkage between the 9/11 attacks and the Iraq War that George W. Bush and his cronies worked so hard to establish. Iraq became a way to show that the idea of American suffering was a narcissistic delusion. How could any weight be given to our suffering when we inflicted so much suffering elsewhere? There was, inevitably, a sense that we deserved to suffer. The Iraq War, like those miserabilist Westerns of the '70s with their vistas of slaughtered Indians, became a way to prove that the U.S. always acts in a way that can't help but provoke others to attack us.

One of the unfortunate strains of American history and American political thought is the inability of some decent, reasonable people to accept the irrational as anything other than anti-intellectual at best and racist at worst. *Ulzana's Raid* does nothing to protect the audience, particularly the white audience, from the intolerable, irresolvable contradiction of thinking of themselves as both guilty and threatened.

Fittingly, the film plays out as a tale of pursuit in which the pursuers are the ones at risk. Ulzana's men drop behind the cavalry in order to stage an attack. When DeBuin wants to push forward to escape the coming onslaught, McIntosh reminds him of the precarious state of their own horses. "Lieutenant," he says, "a horse will run so far, so fast, for so long, and then it will lie down on ya. When a horse lies down on an Apache, he puts a fire under his belly and gets him back on his feet. When the horse dies, he gets off, eats a bit of it, and steals another. Ain't no way you can better that." The parallels to Vietnam are obvious, the white man being drawn to fight an enemy he cannot fathom in a terrain he cannot master no matter the wealth of his resources. But the pursuit can also stand for the distance that separates the warring parties in this movie—a distance that mocks our good intentions.

In the end, Ulzana is dead (significantly, Ke-Ni-Tay is the only one able to kill him), as are his raiding party and most of the cavalry who opposed him. Just as significantly, DeBuin escapes being wounded. In his final exchange with McIntosh, who's been seriously hurt, it remains doubtful if anything will have the ability to shake DeBuin's pure principles, which he now clings to even more fiercely as a way of reckoning with what he's seen. McIntosh, gutshot, is not about to endure the two-days' agony of a wagon ride over rough terrain back to the fort. He will, he knows, bleed out before DeBuin can come back with help, and he will not suffer the indignity of a soldier assigned to stay with him—someone in effect ordered to watch him die. All McIntosh wants is to sit in the shade of his makeshift awning with the makings of a smoke.

McIntosh, you feel, wants to be free of the whole goddamn bunch of them: free of the Apaches, who he knows he has reason to fear; free of the people who cannot comprehend that such a fearsome thing exists in their ordered, rational world. He wants to be rid of savagery and of the well-meaning, pointless disapproval of that savagery.

In its last moments, the movie's stern determination to teach us a hard lesson leaks out, to be replaced instead by a deep, settled sense of despair. McIntosh will die and no one will be there to bury him, and that, he knows, is the way it will be. And still DeBuin can't accept the facts. "It isn't Christian," he almost whispers. "No, it ain't," McIntosh answers.

No. It ain't.

ALOHA AND GOOD NIGHT, TWO BY FLOYD MUTRUX: *ALOHA, BOBBY AND ROSE* AND *AMERICAN HOT WAX*

IF GOD REALLY wanted to show off his work, he'd be a DJ. In the films of Floyd Mutrux, 1975's *Aloha, Bobby and Rose* and 1978's *American Hot Wax*, the music that pours forth from thousands of car radios seemingly tuned to the same station, from portable radios in kitchens and teenage bedrooms and garages—hell, that might be coming out of the air itself—becomes the filigreed settings some unseen creator has chosen to show off the jewels of '70s Los Angeles and 1959 New York City.

The cities might not look like jewels. L.A. is horizontal sprawl and car headlights coming at us through the haze and the sodium glare of the streetlights and billboards. New York isn't the teeming metropolis of Times Square and Broadway, the images that the movies usually give us. The city here is all shadowed, nearly deserted night-time streets. It's as if fifty years after *Drug Store* and *Automat* and *Night Shadows*, Edward Hopper were still working the same territory. Neither L.A. nor New York, as we see them here, are pretty. But they are beautiful. They provide spaces through which the characters move, creating their dramas, finding their places in already existing dramas. What unites the solitary New Yorkers—the teenage girl listening in her Brooklyn bedroom, the fledgling doo-wop group on the street corner, the janitor mopping up a midtown building while the DJ playing the music on his transistor radio works several stories above him, the Los Angelenos shooting pool or pulled into drive-ins or cruising Sunset and Hollywood Boulevard—is the music. The deliberate, unhurried pace of "Bennie and the Jets" complementing the cars cruising Hollywood Boulevard at Sunset. The Drifters' soaring "There Goes My Baby," with a sound and a heart big enough to hold the disappointments and dreams of New Yorkers, from a middle-aged man thinking of his estranged father in Akron, to the teenagers who are listening to the radio and longing for a community they can't imagine but trusting it exists because someone is making music that tells them it does. We are, in these two movies, in the province of night owls, the ones staying up to brood over some lost dream, or the dreamers too keyed up to sleep because, in the next few minutes, they might hear the song, might meet the person, that unlocks all the mysteries. We can let the singer Maria McKee speak for them all:

> During the summer in the late '70s, I never slept. The station I remember was KHJ and KRLA which was an oldies station. The DJ was Art Laboe and they had late-night dedications. Mostly Latino gangbangers calling in to dedicate songs to one another and girls with boyfriends in jail. It was '50s doowop, '60s and '70s soul. Santo and Johnny, Johnny Ace, Jr. Walker and the All-Stars. I was up all night listening to Sad Girl and Puppet and Sleepy dedicate.

Sad Girl. Puppet. Sleepy. Bobby. Rose. Alan. Teenage Louise. These are the denizens of Floyd Mutrux's night town.

OUT IN THE STREETS

It takes only a few minutes of screen time to go from "Begin the Beguine" to "Bennie and the Jets," from '40s glamour to '70s glam, from romantic reverie to the slurred decadent smirk of the Prodigal Son triumphant. Great DJs tell a story by matching moods, rhythms, by allowing the feel of one record to bleed into the next. In that segue from Artie Shaw to Elton John, from low lights to glittery low life, the writer-director Floyd Mutrux lays out the essence of *Aloha, Bobby and Rose.*

At its heart, this is a movie about people who feel the pull of nostalgia before life has given them anything to feel nostalgic about. The movie's lovers are on the lam after a dumb prank ends with a convenience store clerk being shot dead. They're still young but approaching the days when they won't be, and they're knocked out to find, even in these desperate straits, anything resembling romance in their everyday lives, even as they're running to save themselves before the first blushes of that romance have left their cheeks. Bobby (Paul Le Mat), a mechanic working in a garage and barely scraping by, and Rose (Dianne Hull), a single mom still living with her own mother (Martine Bartlett), working in a car wash, and hoping her VW Bug has a few years left in it, are living the kind of lives where you aim to just get through the day free of disaster before falling into bed and starting it all over again in the morning.

Bobby and Rose live in hopes of the ephemeral something better that may lie in their future but remains unrealized in their present. The poignancy of the movie is that as their situation gets worse, those hopes only get keener. *Aloha, Bobby and Rose* opens in a romantic haze with Rose listening to her mother reminisce about some dreamboat from her past. "Oh, honey," she says, "you shoulda seen Hollywood in the '40s." It's the same line used countless times on young people being told what a mistake they made for being born when they were. But here the voice itself seems to arrive from the past, maybe tuned in from the same hazy station playing Artie

Shaw & His Orchestra in the background of the scene. It wavers slightly as if emanating from the ripples and the fading that time has added to the black-and-white photos Rose's mom is poring over in her scrapbook.

Or it could be that the faraway dreaminess of her voice might just be brought on by her afternoon G & T. She remembers parking atop Mulholland with her beau one summer night, feeling like "You could see the valley and the whole rest of the world." And as Rose listens fondly, indulgently, we see her wishing for her own night like this even as she apprehends that her mother's view has now shrunk from the whole rest of the world to the view from her front porch, to the remnants of those memories in the scrapbook lying in her lap. Even as Rose recognizes her mother's refuge in memories, we see her determination to find her own adventures, and maybe even the willfulness to make sure that they wind up being more than memories. Mutrux and his cinematographer, William A. Fraker, shoot the scene in soft afternoon light, a fragile look for fragile memories. And as if to get us used to the abruptness that will inform the rest of the movie, they've no more established the mood then it's gone.

Artie Shaw segues into the familiar lone piano chord that opens "Bennie and the Jets" and we've left memories of Hollywood in the '40s for L.A. in the '70s, watching from overhead the flow of cars cruising Hollywood Boulevard at sunset. "Bennie and the Jets" is holding court on every one of those car radios (inescapable on the air for more than a few minutes in the spring and early summer of 1975, it would have been). And it's sliding out of a jukebox in a dingy downtown L.A. pool parlor where Bobby is hustling some guys. He's not good enough and gets a bust in the chops for not having the dough to settle up a game he's lost. He departs after receiving a promise of more to come if he doesn't have the money by the next night. The threat doesn't stop him and his buddy Moxey (Robert Carradine) from spending the night tooling around town in Bobby's '68 Camaro. The other cars Bobby blows past on the strip—the driver he beats in an impromptu drag race, the drivers who've pulled to the side of the street for coffee or burgers or chili dogs at one of the brutally overlit drive-in joints catering to them—no matter how fast or sleek or gleaming, seem nowhere near powerful enough to contain the coiled desires of their drivers, the wish for release emanating from every sweaty young body we see. At one point Mutrux and Fraker give us a montage of the billboards hovering over Sunset, all of them advertising new albums and upcoming L.A. shows by the Rolling Stones, Marvin Gaye, ELO, Ringo. These are the gods who keeping watching over the scene, the ones communicating with their acolytes over the radio. This same atmosphere was the best thing in Mutrux's debut, *Dusty and Sweets McGee* (1971). But in trying to stay true to the aimlessness of the characters in that semidocumentary story of dopers and junkies trying to get by on the fringes of Los Angeles, Mutrux didn't give the audience anything to hold on to. You could respect his unwillingness to turn the movie into a cautionary tale or an unlikely saga of redemption, respect the director's determination to get at the numbing stasis of junkie life. Dramatically, though, the movie was a punishment to sit through, even as it was easy to recognize in it a street-level view of Los Angeles that recalled some of the shots and sequences in noirs like *Kiss Me Deadly* or *He Walked by Night* or *Murder by Contract*, and the texture of Kent Mackenzie's remarkable *The Exiles*, his 1961 docudrama of Native Americans in the now-destroyed L.A. neighborhood Bunker Hill.

There's no doubt that with *Aloha, Bobby and Rose* Mutrux made a move to a B-movie scenario. To anyone who believes the

unshaped quality of *Dusty and Sweets McGee* is inherently more
truthful than the conventions of genre filmmaking, *Aloha* can't
help but seem a retreat, although the film in no way sacrifices the
feel for place that distinguished the earlier movie. Part of that
achievement was born of necessity. When you're working with a
budget of $60,000, as Mutrux was, you can't afford artifice. But it's
also true that when you set a movie with a feel for the details of
working-class lives within scabbed and scarred real settings—when
you have a director who resists the urge to prettify—then the
simplest travails of the characters, like checking your money before
ordering a take-out meal, can take root, can feel like something
more authentic than just B-movie fatalism. *Aloha, Bobby and Rose* is
a film of echoes and antecedents: Fritz Lang's *You Only Live Once*;
the two superb film versions of Edward Anderson's Depression-era
novel *Thieves Like Us*, the Robert Altman film of that name and
Nicholas Ray's 1948 *They Live by Night*; *Gun Crazy*; the final section
of *Rebel Without a Cause*; inevitably *Bonnie and Clyde*; perhaps
even *Breathless*. But the very willingness to make audiences aware
from the outset that things are not going to turn out well marks it,
like the other films in this book, as a product of a time when
coddling the audience was not a high priority. After Bobby pulls
the stupid stunt that leaves that kid working in the convenience
store dead—pretending to be sticking the kid up and prompting a
nervous old man with a shotgun to emerge from the back room and
hit the young man he's trying to protect—the movie sets up a pull
between Bobby's impulse to run and Rose's insistence that the right
thing to do is to explain what happened to the cops. It's not just
cynicism about authority that causes us, even reluctantly, to side
with him. When Bobby tells Rose that the cops won't believe their
story for a minute, we know he's not speaking out of desperation or

self-pity. This is simply a fact of life for people on the margins, a world in which the cops are not your friends. And it's extraordinary now, more than thirty years after the aesthetic and political conservatism that crept into American movies in the '80s and has never left, to think of a mainstream movie acting on the belief that it wasn't a risk to utter that truth because there existed an audience that would understand and accept it.

For all the ways in which Bobby attempts to run, it's clear, even before that kid is blasted away in front of him, that he isn't going anywhere. Actors' roles can merge in our minds in ways that make them part of one continuous story. Bobby might be a less cocky version of John Milner, the small-town hot-rodder Le Mat played in *American Graffiti* two years earlier. Le Mat is thicker in the face here, and what swagger he's got left is a front. Always late to work, Bobby has to cajole the boss who has had just about enough of him, and he has to humble himself before his car-dealer uncle (Noble Willingham) to ask for the money to settle his pool debt. When Moxey tries to get Bobby to join him in a crash course he's taking, one that will allow a better job when he finishes (better, at least, than the one he has), Bobby tells his buddy that he couldn't face getting up at six A.M. He'd rather get his three hours of sleep after a night out, he says, and start work at noon. Watching *Aloha, Bobby and Rose* in 1975, it was easy enough to see the traces of John Milner in Bobby, easy to see the cockiness leaking out of the hot-rodder who, to his shock, found himself aging. It would take four more years to see the traces of both Bobby and Milner in Le Mat's Melvin Dummar, the Nevada gas station attendant who found himself named a beneficiary in Howard Hughes's "Mormon Will" in Jonathan Demme's 1980 *Melvin and Howard*. There's no bitterness in Le Mat's Melvin, floating from job to job, doing his best to care for his kids and the wives who waft in and out of his life. And there's nothing in Bobby of the optimistic acceptance that Melvin brings to his lot. Bobby isn't yet ready to face up to his dead end, but the traces of resentment are there, the suspicion that he's always going to be dealt a lousy hand and the way he tries to shrug off the resentment by playing the role of the free spirit who hasn't given in to the Man. Which is why, as pliant a performance as Dianne Hull gives, Rose is the stronger one.

Sometimes in the movies, the softer a woman appears, the more the character challenges the audience to look beneath the surface. Has there ever been a *fragile* woman, in the movies or in life, named Rose? It's almost what you name a baby girl to toughen her to life's vicissitudes, the way the no-good father names his son Sue in the Johnny Cash hit. Dianne Hull's Rose, first seen through the soft light used to complement her mother's memories of Hollywood in the '40s, looks like the sort of willowy young thing given to wearing embroidered blouses (she does) and listening to Joni Mitchell (although, along with the other denizens of L.A., Rose seems to be guided through the night by the DJ's mix, happy to listen to whatever he plays). She's the one, though, who instigates the relationship with Bobby, picking him up as he's hitchhiking in the rain (she's told him to wait for a bus after he's returned her repaired VW to the car wash); she's the one who makes him work for the attention she pays him; and, despite her understandable upset by the senseless death of the convenience store clerk, she's the one who insists throughout the movie that they at least consider not running. Hull's acting is unaffected, direct. And in a movie with the sense of fatalism that this one has, her freshness and prettiness carries an implicit tension.

Death hangs over the movie. Scurrying away from the shooting, Bobby pushes Rose into her VW and takes the wheel, which she grabs to turn them around and return to the scene. Before we know it, we're in yet another horror as the abrupt movement sends the car nearly toppling over. Little Eva's "Locomotion," playing on the radio, drowns out everything else on the soundtrack before we register that Fraker and Mutrux have switched to slow motion. Our head-on, through-the-windshield view of Bobby and Rose suddenly tilts, and for a moment it appears to us as if the movie screen itself is titling. We see a web of spider cracks appear on the windshield as each of their heads comes forward to rupture the glass. It's simple but so horrifying, a perfect visual and emotional metaphor for two lives gone off kilter and stained in blood.

Possibly more chilling is the Tijuana idyll the two take with a Texas high roller and his wife (Tim McIntire and Leigh French), who pick up Bobby and Rose following a drive-in altercation with some troublemakers and take them on an impromptu spree. It's a scene of instant boozy familiarity, and the movie needs the variety it provides. We need to be swept up into McIntire's good-ol'-boy generosity and French's dimply hospitality. But the abrupt ending, the four parting after the sudden intrusion of death, prepares us for the inevitability of what's to come.

And on some level we dig the inevitability. For a country said to worship youth, America never loves youth more than when it's doomed. From the outlaw couples of *They Live by Night* and *Gun Crazy* to the misunderstood teens of *Rebel Without a Cause*, from the teen corpses littering death-rock classics like "Leader of the Pack" and "Teen Angel" to the impossibly beautiful young Leonardo DiCaprio and Claire Danes in Baz Luhrmann's *William Shakespeare's Romeo + Juliet*, we know that doom looks gorgeous on the young. You can take that as something necrophilic in our nature, or as a narcissistic mourning for our own lost youth. Or, more generously, you can take it as our ability to recognize the moment when beauty is at its ripest.

Aloha, Bobby and Rose is suspended between two great fantasies: the rock 'n' roll fantasy of the outsiders' romantic wish to find their own paradise, given its grandest, most operatic treatment on Bruce Springsteen's *Born to Run* the same year this movie was released; and the adolescent fantasy of the city as a place where cowboys and Indians has given way to the deadly game of cops and kids. It's that first fantasy, though, from which the movie draws its poignance. You can't dream of paradise unless you recognize the trap in which you're living. *Aloha, Bobby and Rose* marries the idea that animates *Vanishing Point*, *Two-Lane Blacktop*, and *Dirty Mary Crazy Larry*—the idea of speed as a means of escaping the jail of the corporeal—to a story that bears the recognizable details of working-class life. It's a movie about the impulse to run set off in people who are already so close to beat that they just want to stop running, a fantasy of escape and resignation. It's a movie peculiarly suited to the ambiguity of the word *aloha*.

. . . IT'S JUST GOOD NIGHT

It's 1959 and in Mutrux's film *American Hot Wax* the legendary disc jockey Alan Freed is staging his big rock 'n' roll show at Brooklyn's Paramount Theatre. It will be his last—only Freed doesn't know it yet. In the movie's B-melodrama terms, the forces of repression—aka the DA's office, suspicious of kids letting loose, and more specifically, of white kids and black kids letting loose together—are closing in for the kill. And Freed goes down fighting, telling them, "You can stop me. But you can never stop rock 'n' roll."

The real story isn't so pretty. Driven off the air by the payola scandal, hounded by the government for tax evasion, Freed died an alcoholic in 1965 at the age of forty-three—two years more than Tim McIntire, the actor who plays him here, would live to be.

But amid the teeming life of *American Hot Wax*—an urban pop paradise where neon street life beckons outside the windows of homey living rooms, where hucksters hustle people who turn out to have real talent, where songs that will still sound great nearly fifty years later are tossed off as an afternoon's work, where LaVern Baker's hits come effortlessly and a downer like Connie Francis doesn't stand a chance, where every broadcast Alan Freed makes reaches down into teenage bedrooms like messages from the Resistance, where the boundaries that have defined American life (keeping black from white, girls from boys, and dreamers from their dreams) are about to crack wide open—Freed is a hero. In his hipster's checked sports coats and bow ties, his hair slicked back, one hand keeping rhythm to the records he plays while the other alternates between puffs on a Chesterfield and swigs from the bottle of beer that's his on-air companion, Freed is the snap and jive of the music incarnate. But Tim McIntire brings a big man's sadness to the role. His baby-soft jowls make him look remarkably like the man who has long been rumored to be his father, Orson Welles, and his dark-circled eyes hint at the melancholy that he seems to stave off only for the duration of a three-minute pop song. That's the quandary he shares with his listeners. In *American Hot Wax*, the right song at the right moment can wipe away the dross, make sense of the world. But how do you keep that feeling? Freed's sign-off— "It's not good-bye. It's just good night"—is a plea to his listeners to be strong, to keep the faith. "Could they really take all this away, boss?" asks Freed's driver, Mookie (Jay Leno), in the question that hangs over the movie.

With rock 'n' roll a permanent fixture of our culture, pop songs having now replaced the Muzak that used to play in supermarkets, it may strike some people as quaint to think of rock 'n' roll as any threat to the established order. The squares in the movie who are scandalized by Chuck Berry were already comical when the movie was released in 1978. But *American Hot Wax* realizes that the fissures opened by rock 'n' roll, the country's second civil war, have never been smoothed over. It says that the freedom and release and pleasure rock 'n' roll represents can always be taken away. And by making that pleasure synonymous with the very fabric of life, Mutrux made it seem ineffably precious. At times the movie invokes the title of a song by Fairport Convention, a band whose versions of English folk music would have been unthinkable as rock 'n' roll in 1959: "Now Be Thankful."

The joy of *American Hot Wax* is that it accomplishes all this with the verve and energy and spontaneity of B movies. Mutrux lifts the genre proficiency of *Aloha, Bobby and Rose* to a dazzling multistory structure. This is the kind of movie in which you fully expect the life you're watching will continue even after the camera's attention has gone elsewhere. *American Hot Wax* cuts from one narrative thread to another, the characters and their talk crisscrossing the screen as if this is what Robert Altman might have done if he'd made drive-in movies. Life as well as art is improv here. When a doo-wop group assembled for a recording session is beating the life out of "Come Go with Me" with their funereal pace, their producer (played by the record producer Richard Perry, whose long face and lantern jaw make him look like a tough-guy version of the Muppet game-show host Guy Smiley) drags everyone he can find into the studio, from the sandwich delivery boy to the janitor ("You look like you got big hands," he tells the guy) to clap and sing along. Then he turns to the lead singer. "Okay," he says, thinking fast, "we need something here. Give me a dom, dom, dom, dom . . . *dom*. Five *dom*s, and a dom-be-doobie." And presto: doo-wop nirvana.

That scene is about the transformations that lie at the heart of *American Hot Wax.* The three nice, clean-cut kids we see practicing close harmony in a stairwell at the Paramount turn out to be the Fleetwoods, whose aching songs may express the purest longing in all of rock 'n' roll. The ditties that Teenage Louise (Laraine Newman in her moment of big-screen glory as the young Carole King) composes on her family's neglected upright piano turn out to be perfect for the four young black guys who've formed a street-corner doo-wop quartet. (Is there any other kind?)

If Mutrux's direction suggests a B-movie Robert Altman, the screenplay, by screenwriter and novelist John Kaye, suggests Preston Sturges. Kaye loves the glint in the eye that reveals the obsessiveness of ordinary Americans, the mixture of wised-up cynicism and openhearted belief in the patter of everyday speech. Kaye had demonstrated it in his screenplay for the lovely and overlooked road movie *Rafferty and the Gold Dust Twins.* (And he showed an altogether darker grasp of American myth in his indelible diptych of novels *Stars Screaming* and *The Dead Circus.* As portraits of Los Angeles, they can be mentioned in the same breath as Raymond Chandler and Ross Macdonald.) Everybody in this movie—the hip folks, at least—are both streetwise and moonstruck. And Kaye's comedy gets a pair of terrific mouthpieces in Jay Leno's Mookie and Fran Drescher's Sheryl, Freed's secretary. Drescher was twenty-one when the movie was made, and her grating nasal whine hadn't yet become shtick. Here her voice could stand for the abrasiveness and charm of New York City itself. She's never funnier than when the screeching brakes emanating from her vocal cords are affecting propriety as she fends off another of Mookie's klutzy advances. And you can't blame him: She's Selma Diamond reincarnated as a dish. Leno (the promising young comic, as distinct from the late-night glad-hander he became), with that curling mumble mouth in the midst of his absurdly oversized jaw, looks as if the name Mookie might have been invented for him.

In *American Hot Wax*, rock 'n' roll is a pixilated version of democratic pluralism, the only thing that could draw all these disparate people together—even as it draws lines in the dirt between them and others. But if rock 'n' roll provides a home here for people like the twelve-year-old president of the Buddy Holly fan club (Moosie Drier, who shines in the movie's most touching scene) who feel homeless elsewhere, Mutrux and Kaye never let us forget what those folks look like to the movie's arbiters of morality and law. For the DA and his thugs backstage at the Brooklyn Paramount, Chuck Berry, doing the incomparably salacious "Reelin' and Rockin'," is a purveyor of smut. Jerry Lee Lewis, treating the piano as his trampoline, is the most depraved hillbilly imaginable. Screamin' Jay Hawkins? Jesus! A goddamn cannibal, for chrissakes.

And then there's the guy out front.

Out in front of the Paramount, unnoticed by anyone else, oblivious to the excited kids and then to the marauding cops, a homeless black man sits, intent only on banging the cans he's upturned on the sidewalk to provide percussion for his version of "Lucille" and whatever other tune catches his fancy. What would Freed's teen fans see if they noticed him? Some strange colored guy providing a little preshow entertainment. What would the movie's defenders of decency see? A tramp, a bum, "that nigger in the alley," a phrase Curtis Mayfield had sung in another context a few years earlier. But to Mutrux he looks like the spirit of rock 'n' roll itself, making the noise that is always made by anyone who wants to say *I'm here!* A frightened parent's worst nightmare of what will happen to their kids if they listen to rock 'n' roll, he's right out in the open and yet a secret agent. He's the spirit that will sneak its way into crevices and open windows, that will survive Frankie Avalon (or Arcade Fire)—a termite artist, in Manny Farber's phrase. When the DA brings down the curtain, he thinks he's won. What that crazy guy in the street knows is that fighting is in rounds.

STRANGER IN TOWN: *HARD TIMES*

AND THEN THERE'S the cat.

Walter Hill's Depression-era yarn *Hard Times* opens with Chaney, the nearly silent drifter played by Charles Bronson, hopping off a freight train in New Orleans. About a half hour later, he's decided there's some money to be made as a slugger in the town's illicit bare-knuckle boxing bouts. So Chaney does what anybody new to town would do: He finds a place to stay, a room in a shabby residential hotel that rents for twelve bits a week, and goes out for some groceries. When he comes back, along with the coffee and milk and bread, he's got a cat.

Chaney pours her a saucer of milk, which, when she's finished her preliminary exploration of the room, she's happy to lap up. Already she's like her new owner: still not certain this is the place for her, but ready to stay for a while if it means keeping herself fed and having a roof over her head. We tend to associate powerful, muscled guys with dogs. But this kitty is the perfect companion for Chaney: compact, sure of herself, unsentimental, content to go about her own business, making noise only when she needs something.

The bare-knuckle bouts that Chaney takes part in, held surreptitiously in warehouses and on docks, are desperate affairs. No Queensberry Rules here. And since, for some of the boxers, the stakes money is the only thing that stands between them eating and not eating, they are prone to the anger that always puts a boxer off his game. Some, the bald behemoth (Robert Tessier) who has the backing of the local wheeler-dealer, Gandil (Michael McGuire), find a sadistic pleasure in taking apart their opponents.

For Chaney, a boxing match, like everything else, is something to be gotten through with as little fuss as possible. A standard action movie would turn Chaney's first bout into a pugilistic display. It's a measure of how in tune Walter Hill, making his directing debut, is with his stoic hero that Chaney's first bout consists of him shrugging out of his shirt and jacket, decking his opponent with one punch, then putting his clothes back on and leaving. In some ways, *Hard Times* is the story of Charles Bronson leaving one place after another.

Perusing the paper while enjoying a cup of coffee at a late-night sidewalk diner, he gets the attention of the waitress working the graveyard shift and points to his empty mug. "Third refill's a nickel," she tells him. In response, Chaney produces a nickel, says "Tip," and lays it down on the counter before leaving. He knows she needs the nickel more than he needs another cup. When he turns up at the apartment of the washed-out hooker (Jill Ireland) whom he sometimes visits, only to be told she has company, Chaney simply offers her his smile, says, "Some other time," and, with almost ineffable grace, heads back down the stairs. When Speed (James Coburn), the more-cocky-than-bright gambler who backs up Chaney's brawn with money, insults Chaney in a weak moment, Chaney just regards Speed, delivers a one-word verdict—"Dumb"— and takes his leave.

Chaney's a mystery but he's not unreadable. If he's driven by anything, it's a desire to set his own terms and not be burdened with more than he needs. There's none of the action hero's bottled anger in Chaney. No possessiveness or jealousy in relations with women. There's no loose talk, either. In the ninety-four minutes of

Hard Times, Bronson barely makes a peep. He's the star and yet he utters somewhere just south of a thousand words in the whole picture. Chaney takes a foxy delight in not speaking when others most want him to. At the movie's end, he has gotten what he can from the boxing racket and decides it's time to hop back on the freight train. This is the point in nearly any movie where the hero would make his *I'll never forget ya, pal* good-byes to the buddies he's made. Here, when Chaney parts company with Speed and Poe (Strother Martin), the morphine-addicted cut man who tends to his wounds, Speed begs Chaney, "Say *something!*" Chaney only flashes his broad smile, open and enigmatic at the same time, before slipping off into the darkness of the railroad yards.

Throughout the movie Hill brings Chaney face to face with creatures, both human and animal, with whom he passes moments of wordless understanding. The tabby is one. Another is a black bear Chaney finds caged at a riverside Cajun picnic. As cinematographer Philip Lathrop shoots the scene, it's as close to idyllic as these desperate times allow. One shot, a tree to the left of the frame, its branches extending along the top of the frame and dripping Spanish moss like a gauze curtain above the picnickers' heads, could be the work of an American Seurat taking in the leisure of a down-at-the-heels crowd. We don't know why the bear is there. Clearly for someone's cruel amusement. Chaney just regards the animal, it regards him, and there's a flicker in Bronson's eyes of unsentimental compassion. More than any screenwriter's invented backstory, that look tells us that Chaney knows something about constriction. The ease with which Bronson moves through the world, every move graceful, no move wasted, is that of someone who doesn't take his freedom for granted.

In a time when the conditions of life itself felt like a trap to so many, Chaney's commitment to freedom feels like his means of self-respect. In a lovely moment that occurs under the titles, Chaney stands at the open door of the freight train car bringing him to New Orleans. As the train passes a railroad crossing he sees two children standing in the back of a battered family pickup, their parents in the cab. Like him, those kids are the travelers the Depression set on the road, and like him, they don't know where they're heading. They hold each other's gaze as the train moves by, and what passes between them is both guarded—people on the road cannot afford to trust easily—and the gravest respect of travelers who recognize each other's uncertain futures.

Throughout his film career, Bronson was most at home in the realm of the stoic and the taciturn. But at least until the success of *Death Wish* trapped him in one vigilante role after another, he possessed an instinctive sense of how the camera magnifies gestures and changes of expression. Bronson could sketch in a character's emotions in a way that seemed both spare and hearty. Starting out as a bit player in the '50s, Bronson—then acting under his real name of Charles Buchinski—was memorable as the polite hood who turns down Spencer Tracy's offer of a glass of buttermilk in *Pat and Mike* by explaining, "It gives me the gas." And he brought something pitiable to the standard horror film role of madman's mute assistant in the 3-D outing *House of Wax*. In the '60s, Bronson was often part of ensemble action spectacles like *The Magnificent Seven* and (the best of these) *The Great Escape*. In that film Bronson plays a Polish flight lieutenant in a German POW camp who fights his own claustrophobia to dig an escape tunnel. The director, John Sturges, juxtaposes Bronson's bravery with his vulnerability in a way that allows the audience to feel the man's wounded dignity. Bronson closed out the decade as Harmonica, the silent center of Sergio Leone's staggering *Once Upon a Time in the West*. Like the other actors in Leone's film, Bronson is given overpowering Panavision close-ups meant to etch the faces in your mind as permanently as the faces carved on Mount Rushmore.

The tension in Bronson's screen presence came from the contradiction between the wide closed-mouth grin that creased his face and the narrow eyes that never gave much away. In the first fight scene of *Hard Times* the smart-aleck young slugger he faces looks him over and says, "You're a little old for this game, ain't you, Pops?" There's a cheerful murderousness lurking in the smile Chaney gives in return. Bronson never suggests a man in danger of losing control but one for whom control is never in question. He seems like the sort of solid workingman of immigrant stock who learned early on not to give away too much of what he was thinking. He could be very likable, as in *Mr. Majestyk*, as the melon farmer defying the gangsters out to stop him from bringing in his crop. But Bronson frequently suggested that it was smart to be wary around him. His final moments in the 1986 HBO docudrama *Act of Vengeance* best capture his power. Bronson played Joseph Yablonski, the labor leader who ran for president of the United Mine Workers only to be murdered as he slept, along with his wife and daughter, on orders from the UMW's then president Tony Boyle. Mortally wounded in his bed, with the corpse of his wife beside him, Bronson's Yablonski rises up to stare down his killers and, as if the man were already dead and his ghost were coming from the grave to shred them nerve from nerve, the killers flee in terror.

In *Hard Times* Bronson's reserve plays off James Coburn's bravado. If Chaney keeps his mouth shut when he grins, Coburn makes you feel you can see every chopper in his skull, right back to the rear molars. Speed's nickname comes from his inability to keep from running off at the mouth. He can't accept victory gracefully: He's got to rub his opponents' noses in it. It's bad enough that he owes the local loan shark (Bruce Glover, an actor whose perverse menace has something to do with the way his features seem too small for his wide face); Speed doesn't have the sense to keep a low profile. First he has to raise a bundle to put Chaney up against Gandil's top slugger. Then, when Chaney wins the bout and makes back the investment times three, Speed blows his share in a craps game before even stopping at the shark's to pay back his debt. Speed is the kind of goddamn fool you can't help but like, and Coburn, usually so cool a screen presence, shows a lack of vanity by putting his considerable charisma at the service of playing this fool.

By the time *Hard Times* opened in 1975, the Depression had become a familiar milieu in American movies, particularly gangster movies. *Bonnie and Clyde* (1967) presented the era at ironic distance—misread by many critics as romanticized—that aimed to capture the place the era had come to occupy in American mythology. Nothing so ambitious was attempted in the Depression-set gangster films that followed—*Dillinger, The Grissom Gang, Bloody Mama, The Moonshine War*—until Robert Altman, adapting Edward Anderson's 1937 novel, *Thieves Like Us*, infused it with the flavor of William Faulkner. Many of the cinematic depictions of the Depression, especially Peter Bogdanovich's 1973 *Paper Moon*, took their visual clues from the photographs of Walker Evans, Dorothea Lange, and the other WPA photographers. *Hard Times*, as shot by Philip Lathrop, seems to take its cues from painters. There is, inevitably in a film that aims to reproduce the desperation of the era when some measure of life has seemingly leaked out of even New Orleans, a touch of Edward

Hopper. But it's other painters the film calls to mind. The faces of the girls in the brothel Speed visits, and especially the big-eyed blonde whom Poe cuddles up to on the dance floor as if she were mother and lover in one, recall the painted faces of the painted ladies, garish and eager or just too worn out to care, in the canvases of Reginald Marsh. And, of course, for a boxing movie, the spirit of George Bellows is present—not only for his boxing pictures (the mixture of poetic realism and journalistic hard edge you see in the most famous of them, *Dempsey and Firpo*) but for the spare and weathered city spaces of *Blue Morning* and *Excavation*, depicting the construction of Penn Station. These are paintings in which people sit idly by a project as if they have lost their purpose or, as in *Excavation*, are not present at all. These canvases are distinct from the teeming life in Bellows's portraits of poor neighborhoods or boys gathering on a city dock to go skinny-dipping. In these canvases, the structures have overwhelmed the life that exists, just as in *Hard Times* battered public spaces persist even though the life they are meant to serve has emptied out.

Except for Gandil's waterfront oyster-shucking business, where we see men stand behind rough wooden tables from beneath which piles of empty oyster shells spill as if from a cave, we have no idea if any of the factories we see in the movie are still in use. They're part of a social and economic structure that seems forgotten, leaving these street fighters and the gamblers betting on them free to make use of them in the deserted New Orleans night. Several times during one of the sequences set in the factory, Lathrop cuts to an extreme high shot, filmed from above both the fighters and the spectators ringing the space around them. The entire scene suddenly seems as lonely as the nighttime street corner past which a lone pedestrian makes his way in the Edward Hopper etching.

In its trim, pulp fashion, in the taciturnity of its hero, in the semideserted feel of its urban settings, *Hard Times* insists on a solitude that defined the '30s, unlike the solidarity of the decade that would follow, when economic desolation was replaced by the common purpose of a country at war. The '30s was a decade in which the musical question "Brother, Can You Spare a Dime?" was asked with no guarantee of an answer. Chaney is ahead of the game because as a loner he's at home in a time when everybody is on their own.

But if this beautifully directed movie has been whittled down, it also feels like one with room to breathe. When Speed goes to hunt down Poe to tend to Chaney's cuts and bruises, he finds him in a black church, and Hill gives us a minute to take in the small choir, to note the gravity and respectability of the singers, the men with their hair shaved high on the sides and the women with simple, almost prim processes. Instead of stuffing the movie with boxing scenes, they are paced far apart and each one serves to advance the story, to define the changes in Chaney and Poe's business friendship. It's a modest movie and, for the work of a first-time director, amazingly assured. And yet the texture and mood of the era it recreates, so unobtrusively yet so deeply, sinks into your bones and makes you feel you've been given some essential knowledge of the time it depicts.

The twist of this movie celebrating a loner hero is that it climaxes with an unexpected recognition of commonality. Gandil, angry that his slugger has lost to Chaney and that Chaney won't come to work for him, brings in a ringer to win back his lost dough and to put Chaney out of commission. The guy who arrives in town to do the job is an arrogant type, several degrees slicker than anyone else in the movie. And of course Chaney beats him. Their bout is the longest in the film, and the roughest, not just to prolong the suspense of who will win, but to define Chaney's essence. When Chaney finally gets the upper hand—when the sharpster who comes close to beating him is on the ground, unable to get up— Hill gives us a moment of Chaney seeing his opponent no longer as a threat but as the man he might be, the guy who goes down in defeat looking for some measure of mercy. He sees himself. And you know, in that moment, Chaney is at the end of the fight game. His work is done. All that's left, before hopping a freight out of town, is to slip Poe some money and tell him to take care of the cat.

E PLURIBUS LOONUM: CITIZENS BAND

IN AMERICAN COMEDY, the cuckoo is often indistinguishable from the optimist. Ignoring obstacles, or more likely not knowing they exist, the cuckoo strides through life with the blithe confidence that the most cracked schemes can become reality. In the great screwball comedies America is very much the Land of Opportunity, but the Land of Opportunity as seen in a fun-house mirror. Which is why the nuttiest schemes its dreamers can dream up often come true. Carole Lombard's ditzy rich girl in *My Man Godfrey* (1936) sees no reason why William Powell, as the forgotten man who's unwittingly won her patronage, can't move overnight from the riverside dump adjoining Sutton Place into the mansions lining the streets. She looks at a bum and sees a butler and a husband. She exudes the sense that walking through life six inches off the ground has lifted her into a place where the oxygen has been replaced by ether. And although she doesn't have a whit of the common sense or experience that Powell's Godfrey has in spades, she's got confidence. There's a will of iron behind Lombard's breathless exclamations.

Cuckoos span the social classes. The Rotary Clubs and ladies' auxiliaries of Preston Sturges's *The Miracle of Morgan's Creek* and *Hail the Conquering Hero* are full of them. And so is Union, the felicitously named working-class town of Jonathan Demme's 1977 *Citizens Band.* Among them is the lantern-jawed character actor Charles Napier as the sort of gung-ho optimist whom Carole Lombard's society girl would have recognized as a country cousin.

Napier plays a happy, horny trucker who goes by the handle the Chrome Angel. One of the regular rest stops for this king of the road is the home of Hot Coffee (played by the ineffable Alix Elias), a squeaky-voiced, curly-haired hooker, who for years has been offering passing truckers like the Angel what she calls her "hundred-mile perk-me-up." But, she explains, what with the new highway offering a quicker route, business has fallen off and she's not sure what she's going to do. She needn't worry. The gleam in the Angel's eye is as unwavering as the romantic mist in Lombard's when she first sets her peepers on Powell. "The whole country is going mobile," the Angel tells her, "and if you can get behind that, you can do anything!" And soon, courtesy of the down payment the Angel makes on a spiffy new RV, Hot Coffee is proving him right, plying her trade on the highways, using her CB to call out to the surprised truckers who don't think they have time for one of her perk-me-ups—until they spot her in their rearview mirrors.

The laughs in *Citizens Band*, its genuine delight in the oddity of ordinary people and its faith in their ability to do the right thing, spring from the comedy of eternal American reinvention. Mobility is partly the source of that reinvention, the mobility of truckers and those, like Hot Coffee, who serve them. But the movie's hero, Spider (Paul Le Mat), is stationary, and his predicament provides a core of pain beneath the comedy.

Spider has set up and operates a CB radio mobile reac unit from his home, allowing him to act as a conduit for people in emergencies (like the Chrome Angel, whose eighteen-wheeler skids off the road one night while he's distracted by some dirty talk coming over the CB). It's a volunteer gig that gets him honored by the local VFW yet doesn't change much else in his life. Spider lives in a rural version of *Sanford and Son*'s Watts junkyard, a drab, run-down house with rusted-out autos and other detritus littering the scabby grounds. He shares the place with his father (the lovely Canadian actor Roberts Blossom, so frail and tremulous a presence, his own ghost seems to be hovering a few inches behind him), a retired trucker who goes by the handle Papa Thermodyne and who comes out of his depressed stupor only when a trucker who still remembers him rouses him on the CB. When the radio is silent, the old man can barely emit a whisper to answer when Spider asks him how he slept or if his coffee is okay.

There are three other sons: One is in prison, one is off on his own, and another, Roy (Bruce McGill), is a high school basketball coach who won't come near the place. So Spider is stuck, and Le Mat, a wonderful actor who never had the career he should have, emits a kind of eager friendliness that seems a mask for the wounds and restlessness underneath. It's an indication of how keen a grip Demme has on the overall comic tone that the scenes between Le Mat and Blossom don't throw the movie out of whack. You feel the needy boy in Spider reaching out to his daddy only to find an absence. In one scene Spider comes home to find his father passed out drunk and can do no more than weep over the old man. And so, after being unable to clear a radio line when a pilot makes an emergency landing on the highway in front of him, and needing something in his life, Spider goes on a vigilante crusade to shut down the abusers clogging up the CB's emergency channels. It says something about the movie's loopy heart that it takes family pain seriously but treats Spider's vigilante exploits as lighthearted farce. When he forces his way into a suburban home to smash the CB radio of a kid consistently abusing the emergency channels, the kid's mother thanks Spider for doing what she's been longing to.

By the time *Citizens Band* came out, CB radios, long in use by truckers and police and fire and ambulance services, had become a craze among much of the rest of America. Their popularity produced C. W. McCall's terrible novelty song "Convoy" in 1975 and Sam Peckinpah's affable road movie of the same name in 1978. You could buy guides to help you learn CB lingo the way you could buy them to help you learn to disco dance. These were manuals for the people who'd soon be on to the next fad, books that were destined to turn up at yard sales for the next few years.

The CB is what links all the characters in *Citizens Band*, the ones who depend on it, like Spider and the Chrome Angel and Hot Coffee, as well as the dabblers. The screenwriter, Paul Brickman, hit upon a simple realization—that CB radio, on which you were expected to adopt a persona, allowed people not just to live out their fantasy lives but to broadcast those fantasies to an audience who could talk back. And so, in *Citizens Band*, the nerdy young man too shy to make it with girls can dub himself Warlock and carry on radio sex with Electra (Candy Clark), who in reality is Pam, the high school girls' gym teacher who used to be Spider's fiancée. (Your heart goes out to the poor schlub when he has to cut a steamy session short because he needs to return his father's sedan.) An even nerdier high schooler, who can't be more than thirteen or fourteen, finds that, on the air, his red hair, baby fat, and owlish glasses don't matter. He can just call himself the Hustler and boasts of all the girls he's had. There are some people who aren't as interested in talking to as talking at: an old woman provides endless droning monologues about her nineteenth-century prairie girlhood. She's Laura Ingalls Wilder with logorrhea. And there's a Nazi (the blue-eyed '70s fixture Harry Northrup) who sells Der Führer as a good ol' boy. But even he's not so much a threat as just one more screwball in the melting pot.

The great, resonant joke of *Citizens Band* is that the fantasy lives of these ordinary Americans are so close to the surface. These people don't need to be drawn out or encouraged, just given an alias and a microphone. When the characters are identified in the end credits, it's by their CB handles, not their names. Those crazy identities, Demme and Brickman are saying, may just be their truest selves. Even Spider's vigilante campaign doesn't change their habits. They're still prattling the same nonsense at the end. The movie isn't out to punish its characters for indulging their fantasies; Demme and Brickman realize how important those fantasies are. These characters need their fantasies. Without the role of the beloved Papa Thermodyne, Spider's dad is just an old drunk rambling around his dump of a home in a tattered bathrobe. That old woman who goes on about her girlhood looks to have outlived (or just worn out) the friends and family she probably used to bore with her tales. Warlock and Electra, who'd never get together in real life, have a fantastic time making it over the radio because each one allows the other to be the sexy person they can't be in the everyday world. The movie's idea of a happy ending is one that allows these fantasies to be wedded to real life. When Pam and Spider make up at the end of the movie—after he's discovered her secret radio life—she woos him as Electra. "There are a lot of voices out there," she whispers seductively to him. "But yours is different. I like it."

Jonathan Demme worked as a movie publicist before enrolling in the B-movie film school of Roger Corman's New World Pictures. There he directed his first feature, *Caged Heat*, a women's-prison picture revered by those who love the genre. The casting revealed the director's cinephilia. One of the inmates was played by Erica Gavin, star of Russ Meyer's X-rated hit *Vixen!* (Napier, who appeared in nearly every Demme film until his death in 2011, was another Meyer veteran.) And the wheelchair-bound warden, who gets to tap-dance in a surrealistic dream sequence, was played by

Barbara Steele, the British actress whose face memorably went into an iron maiden in Mario Bava's *Black Sunday*. *Citizens Band* was Demme's fourth feature, after the gangster outing *Crazy Mama* and the vigilante picture *Fighting Mad*, and it marked the direction his career would take for some years to come.

Citizens Band was the beginning of Demme's love affair with American outcasts, and the first film in which he demonstrated his effortless feel for the pleasures and hardships of hardscrabble working-class life. That theme would find its most lyrical expressions in two films, 1980's *Melvin and Howard*, again starring Paul Le Mat, a true American tall tale about Melvin Dummar, the trucker named as a beneficiary of Howard Hughes's will, and the 1984 *Swing Shift*, starring Goldie Hawn as a military wife who takes a job in a California airplane factory during World War II and falls in love with a jazz trumpeter (Kurt Russell). *Swing Shift* is Demme's masterpiece—except that nobody knows it because almost no one has seen the movie as Demme intended it. What they have seen is the version released to theaters, taken away from Demme by Hawn, the star and producer who had final approval over the picture; it was recut, reportedly under the direction of Hawn and her producing partner Anthea Sylbert. The bootleg of Demme's original cut, which was passed around among film critics like samizdat for years, makes nonsense of the claims put out by Hawn and Sylbert that Demme's version lacked focus and they were simply rescuing a production in trouble.*

---

*The whole rotten story, along with a fine critical appreciation of Demme's delicate and vandalized work, is told by the critic Steve Vineberg in his "Swing Shift: A Tale of Hollywood" in the Winter 1990–91 issue of *Sight and Sound*.

The love of everyday weirdness, the texture of middle-class and working-class lives, made Demme, for a time, the natural heir to Preston Sturges. But Sturges's great films took place in a time when the country was coming together to fight World War II. And, with the exception of *Swing Shift*, which takes place in that same era, Demme's comedies from *Citizens Band* to 1986's *Something Wild*, six years into the ongoing Republican campaign to turn America into an oligarchy, take place in a more precarious time, when the idea of community was becoming more and more fractured.

The town in *Citizens Band* is one of those places stuck somewhere between working-class and rural. There are bars and diners. There's the same Chinese restaurant that's in every small town. There's some nondescript apartment houses and some nicer suburban homes. But none of it has any character; no one seems particularly connected to the place. This is either where they've wound up or where they've never bothered to leave. But it's no accident that the town is called Union. The community here is found on the go, in the connections between Hot Coffee and her customers; between the drivers in distress and Spider, who helps them out; between Papa Thermodyne and the truckers who call him when they're in range of his CB. If life is impermanent, it also has the virtue of adaptability. The looniest, sweetest demonstration plays itself out in the Chrome Angel's story. The broken arm he suffers in his accident sidelines him, and his wife (Marcia Rodd)—worried about him and maybe convinced he's playing around—hops on the bus from Portland to check up on him. On the ride down she meets a chatty, giggly redhead (Ann Wedgeworth) from Dallas who, like her, has two kids and is married to a trucker. As it turns out, the same trucker. The Angel has been leading a double life and now he's been found out.

The resolution is a measure of the movie's generous, goofy soul. The women agree to meet their bigamist hubby for a powwow—in Hot Coffee's RV. Savor that: Two women, discovering they're married to the same trucker, meet up with him to talk about a way forward in the RV of a traveling hooker (although they don't know what she does or that their husband is one of her regulars). And it's Hot Coffee who provides the answer. After listening to the trio cry and argue through the afternoon, keeping them plied with cups of her famous Vienna Roast all the while, she decides to offer her view. None of them would even be talking, she figures, if they didn't really love each other. So wouldn't it make sense to try it out? "Maybe not in the same house," she says, "but a duplex doesn't seem so bad." And a few minutes later the Chrome Angel, his Dallas Angel on one side, and his Portland Angel on the other are walking off, arms around each other, to their motel and a new future.

The final scenes of *Citizens Band* give Union a chance to live up to its name. First, there's a search for Papa Thermodyne after he's had enough and takes off for Canada. It's a great sequence: All the characters come together (even the Nazi, casting aspersions on everyone around him, but searching nonetheless) and, with the use of the gadget that connected them in the first place, locate their wandering old trucker. Then there's Spider and Electra's wedding, conducted with the bride and groom in separate cars while a preacher, driving a third, conducts the service over the CB.

It might be tempting to look at *Citizens Band* now, almost forty years after its release, and see a harbinger of the way the digital age has let loose people's hidden personalities. But there are crucial differences. CBs add what texting and e-mail and instant messaging delete: an immediate human presence. Hearing the voice of another person prevents the inevitable misreadings of tone that characterize online communication, allowing you to hear, right away, the effect of your words on the person you are talking to. The characters in *Citizens Band* can assume identities, but their voices don't lie. The errant ones here are the ones indulging in monologues and not dialogues, the ones who hog the technology and keep it from its intended purposes to help out people in a jam.

And the short distances that limit CB communication play a part, too. At bottom this is a movie in which people passing through each other's lives are determined to be helpful if they can, or at least genial. Its message could come from another movie Roberts Blossom appeared in that same year, *Close Encounters of the Third Kind*. In that picture he's a true believer in the existence of UFOs, regaling a meeting of the like-minded with the tale of the time he saw Bigfoot. But when we first see him, he's standing on a mountain road, waiting for the ships that he knows are coming. He's even made a sign to greet the beings inside. On it are four words that sum up optimistic American friendliness, whether to aliens or to the guy putting the hammer down on the interstate: STOP AND BE FRIENDLY.

THE GOOSING OF THE PRESIDENT:
WINTER KILLS

"**TUCSON.**" **THAT'S ALL** the aging mobster needs to say. The contempt in his voice conveys the weary disgust of every sharpster who's ever found himself stuck in Hicksville. What can you say about a place where the menu features Wild West Pastrami? The only way to even guess what city we're in *this* time is by the bleeding colors of the Sierra Club sunset on the backdrop outside the fake window.

Otherwise we're in the same dingy hotel room that hundreds of old movies on late-night TV have landed us in before. Rooms where bad men set up a job or hide out after one. Only this time the players know they're reaching the end of the line. "Older, fatter, uglier." That's how Gameboy Baker describes himself, his silk robe and black dress socks making him look less like a slick operator in repose than an old man running to paunch in his accustomed, soon-to-be-outmoded style. And Joe Diamond, in his plaid sports jacket and cream-colored fedora? He could be a Miami retiree headed out to a night at the poker tables.

They're not going to be pulling jobs much longer, and this one doesn't even make sense. We might have known it'd be a hit. *But on the president?* When Gameboy reveals who the target is, it scares Joe so badly that he falls to his knees—and all Joe has to do is shoot the shooter. "Why me?" Joe wonders. Sure, he owes Gameboy, who set him up in his club. And sure, he stole from Manny and Sal and Uncle Louie, but he always intended to pay them back. The pastrami and celery tonic sitting in his stomach is bad enough, but screw the pastrami. This is setting off a worse fire in his guts. The president? Are they crazy? And why does Gameboy talk as if it's just another job, as if the president were just another chiseler destined to wind up in a landfill or in the trunk of a stolen car? This isn't how business is supposed to proceed.

But then, *Winter Kills* isn't how a movie was supposed to proceed, either. In the late '70s you didn't go out to see Ralph Meeker (as Gameboy Baker) or Eli Wallach (as Joe Diamond) playing the kind of scene familiar from endless late nights slumped in front of the TV flicking the remote. And you sure as hell didn't expect JFK's assassination in the midst of some worn-out gangster picture. It's as if *The Late Show* had been introduced with the words that in the '60s heralded so much unthinkable news: "We interrupt this program to bring you a special report . . ."

That sense of dislocation, the feeling of seeing the familiar unfold in a fun-house mirror, is the very air of the conspiracy-theory burlesque *Winter Kills*, which came and went from theaters in one week in the spring of 1979. Less than sixteen years after JFK's assassination, here was a picture that treated the legends and gossip and theories that had sprung up around the killing as some insanely complicated joke, less national trauma than national tall tale. In the days before home video, the picture's very existence could feel like a rumor, even if you had seen it. I did: I was one of three people watching the Sunday-night late show in a suburban shopping mall two-plex. (It was either that or the offering across the way, *Firepower*, featuring James Coburn, Sophia Loren, and O. J. Simpson.) For years after, I kept wondering if I had really seen it. Surely I had imagined Elizabeth Taylor and Toshiro Mifune in the same movie? Or John Huston striding across the screen in a

samurai robe and red bikini underwear? Or the presence of so
many Hollywood faces who weren't seen in the new Hollywood of
the '70s—Dorothy Malone? Richard Boone?

The movie, directed by William Richert and adapted from the
novel by Richard Condon, takes the form of a baroque snipe hunt
in which the dead president's half brother Nick Kegan (Jeff Bridges)
is set on the track of every new conspiracy, every scrap of information whispered in his ear. Nick's fall down the rabbit hole begins
when he hears a dying man's confession that he was the second gun
in the assassination eighteen years before. The scene takes place on
an oil tanker at sea with Vilmos Zsigmond's camera imitating the
roll of the ocean. This is the metaphorically shaky ground Nick will
find himself on for the rest of the movie, and the source of its
comedy.

Nick careens from insane tycoons playing war games on their
property to corrupt cops turned chicken farmers to pinstripe-suited
hoods conducting business in the back of a neighborhood bakery to
all manner of informers and flunkies and crackpots. Richert takes
the snakes' nest of entanglements that Oliver Stone would present
with po-faced urgency in *JFK* and tosses it all off with a cackle.
Politicians and businessmen in bed with the mob? Of course they
are. Witnesses dying in defiance of the odds and the actuarial
tables? Like clockwork. Those collisions—of history and myth-
making, of muckraking and gossip, of the different eras and
genres of American movies—are part of the deliberate design of
Winter Kills.

By 1979 the glamour of the Kennedy years had been sweated
off. Not just by withering assessments of JFK's cold-war adven-
turing and his administration's timidity on civil rights. But by
the stories of consorting with gangsters; of votes bought and

paid for by old Joe Kennedy, bootlegger, ambassador to the Court of St. James's, advocate of appeasing Hitler; by the stories of assassination attempts on Castro coming out of the Senate's Church Commission; by tales of JFK's womanizing that seemed less honest carnality than frat-boy sport fucking. It was as if America's attitude towards JFK had gone straight from the hero worship of Galbraith and Schlesinger to the *National Enquirer*.

If JFK's legacy and image were up for grabs, so was his assassination. What figures like Jim Garrison and Mark Lane had been claiming for years seemed to have seeped, like osmosis, into the consciousness of Americans, 87 percent of whom, according to a 1976 *Detroit News* poll, didn't believe that Lee Harvey Oswald had acted alone. The next year the House Select Committee on Assassinations released a report saying the president was probably killed as a result of a conspiracy but that a second gunman could not be identified. JFK's death was now seen in light of the cynicism that followed Watergate, less a shock than dirty business as usual. Hitting a pitch of dogged delirium in his essay "A Harlot High and Low," Norman Mailer would even look to link Watergate to an attempt to prevent the leak of information about the assassination.

"What a crazy country we inhabit," Mailer writes at the end, throwing up his hands. "What a harlot. What a brute. She squashes sausage out of the minds of novelists on their hotfooted way to a real good plot."

Instead of feeling frustrated by the way the assassination conspiracies didn't cohere, Richert saw that lack of cohesion as an opportunity. He realized that all our national obsessions—politics, show biz, organized crime, sex, scandal, the rich—came together in the Kennedy assassination. Here was a story that was just as at home in *People* as in *Time*, as well as in those downscale markets that

Henry Luce's organization wouldn't sully their hands with. The picture calls up good gossip and social legends. When Nick's girlfriend (Belinda Bauer) is told she can't enter a fancy Manhattan restaurant in trousers, she whips them off, hands them to the maître d', and strides to her table in jacket and nylons—which is exactly what the socialite Nan Kempner did when some hapless boob tried to keep her from entering the dining room of La Côte Basque because of her Yves Saint Laurent pantsuit. The movie is awash in polished mahogany and marble, plushly decorated interiors, swank restaurants, and expensive, well-tailored clothes. If this is a viper's nest, it's one in which we'd be willing to take our chances.

Following Nixon's pardon and the country-club prison sentences handed out to the Watergate conspirators, Americans were no longer certain that the guilty and corrupt would pay for their crimes. That didn't mean they had stopped expecting answers. Somebody was responsible for killing JFK and they still believed it was possible to find out who. But even if it were possible to find out who did it, would we want to know? No answer could be as good as a conspiracy in which the connections got wilder and more sinister. So, in *Winter Kills*, Richert serves up conspiracy theory upon conspiracy theory, each one making hash of the previous tale. He takes all the rumors, facts, myths, and theories and proceeds to squash out the tastiest sausage of all.

The underside of the extraordinary achievements of American movies in the '70s was the paranoid hopelessness in which many of them were drowning. Following Vietnam and Watergate, it was acceptable to treat the Kennedy assassination as fodder for potboiler "exposés" like *Executive Action* (1973) or, in a much better movie, the *The Parallax View* (1974), as what the dark and shadowy "they" would always get away with.

In some ways *Winter Kills* mirrors that hopelessness in a way that a much darker and much better movie, also taken from a Richard Condon novel, John Frankenheimer's 1962 *The Manchurian Candidate*, does not. There is more of the Kennedy assassination in Frankenheimer's film, even though it was made the year before Kennedy's murder—not because the murders that end that film foreshadow President Kennedy's fate, as some have claimed, but because they carry with them the shock of sudden death. The difference is that in *The Manchurian Candidate*, along with that shock comes pleasure: the pleasure of seeing those enemies of the Republic who thought themselves untouchable finally get theirs.

Winter Kills doesn't confront us with anything like that mixture of exhilaration and horror. *The Manchurian Candidate* is a movie about the tragedy of hope.

Winter Kills, on the other hand, is about the comedy of political calcification. Richert is tweaking an America that demands answers and actions all the while ready to cede victory to the rich and powerful, who, we assume, will take it anyway.

Instead of wallowing in hopelessness, Richert saw the mythology that had grown up around the assassination as a manifestation of the American cuckoo. Richert treats the mobsters and industrialists and corrupt cops who inhabit the story that followed the assassination as sleazy versions of the homegrown American oddballs who populate screwball comedy. Except for Anthony Perkins, who, as always, is on his own wavelength. Blanketed in a soft white suit a size too big for him, prowling a catwalk at the top of the Kegan family information silo, he's Cerruti, the master of his own fiefdom of dirty facts. If J. Edgar Hoover, with his meticulous files, was the bulldog of damning information, Perkins is the tic-ridden whelp.

At the perplexed center of this band of grotesques, Bridges has the slightly obdurate handsomeness of a college football player. He's too appealing to be a patsy but a bit too callow to be the hero. Bridges uses his smooth good looks as a sleek joke on Nick's incomprehension. Nick wants it all to make sense, and it's that naïve optimism that's the movie's target.

The dead president's foolishness, Cerruti tells Nick, was acting as if he were presiding over a democracy. And no one represents the vested interests more than John Huston's Pa Kegan. Looking enormous, with a face more like a rock formation than anything else, Huston is appallingly funny in a way that the self-satisfied grotesquerie of Roman Polanski's *Chinatown* did not allow. In whatever scene he marches into, Huston is ridiculous, but you're struck by his sheer chutzpah. No matter where Nick's investigation takes him, he always finds his father's imprint. If Nick takes his lover, Yvette (Belinda Bauer), to lunch at a fancy restaurant, it turns out Pa has the place bugged. Too many important people making deals for Pa Kegan not to listen in.

The old man has his hands in oil drilling, Hollywood studios, banks, and, when his murdered son was campaigning for the White House, buying votes. To Pa Kegan, that's just another way of doing business: You lay out the money you have to in order to ensure a return on your investment. He's the all-American son of a bitch who in his own foul and larcenous way believes himself something like a tougher-minded Horatio Alger. And Richert gives him a spectacular exit.

Clinging to the enormous American flag flying from the Kegan corporate headquarters, Pa Kegan falls to his death among the folds of Old Glory, literally rending it in two on his way to the sidewalk below.

The loss of American innocence has been claimed so many times now that it's a little like an oft-married bride choosing to wear white. We don't have to believe that America was ever innocent (nor the concomitant lie that we are always guilty) to allow for the shocks that have seeped into the fabric of our national lives. And after the one-two punch of Vietnam and Watergate, the myth of Camelot may have looked more attractive than ever.

And so part of the lift of *Winter Kills* is the naughty thrill of laughing at what we think we shouldn't. Richert knows that along with public tragedy comes a self-imposed public silence, an internal mechanism that tells us not to think, much less speak, ill of the dead. The movie gives us permission to acknowledge and to laugh at the sheer trashiness of what made the Kennedy White House seem less like Camelot than Vegas East: Judith Exner and Sam Giancana, Jack and Bobby reportedly passing Marilyn Monroe between them. When Elizabeth Taylor, herself the perfect embodiment of celebrity glamour and tabloid scandal, shows up plump and ripe in a silent cameo as the late president's procuress, the picture achieves some sort of gossipy kismet. It also captures, thanks to Robert Boyle's production design and the burnished chill of Zsigmond's cinematography, our fantasies of the plumminess and spaciousness of the abodes of the rich.

Assembling the kind of oddball cast that Quentin Tarantino would later make his specialty, Richert, remarkably for a first-time director, managed to lasso not just Bridges (still establishing himself as a leading man) but John Huston, Anthony Perkins, Richard Boone (faithfully drunk for each day of shooting), Sterling Hayden (who lit up a big meerschaum pipe packed with dope when Richert met him to discuss the script in the bar of the Beverly Hills Hotel), Toshiro Mifune, Dorothy Malone (as Nick's sweet, elegant drunk

of a mother, inexpressibly fragile and touching in her one scene
with Bridges), Ralph Meeker, Eli Wallach, and Taylor (who tried to
wrangle Richert out of the fur her character wears, in addition to
the $100,000 she earned for a week's work). Richert demonstrates a
fan's delight and a lucky director's shrewdness. He's clearly tickled
to be working with all these people, and they—as if finding themselves at some cheerfully disreputable tea party—all dig in as if they
knew they were doing something really nifty and might not get the
chance again.

They nearly didn't get this chance. To hear Richert tell the
story of the film's making, as he did a few years back during a
retrospective of his work at the Film Society of Lincoln Center and
in the documentary *Who Killed* Winter Kills?, which accompanies
the now-deleted Anchor Bay DVD, is to hear a story as crazy as the
film he made.

Winter Kills was shut down three times during production
when there was no money to continue. The producers, Leonard J.
Goldberg and Robert Sterling, whose biggest success had been the
exploitation hit *Black Emmanuelle*, were reportedly financing the
film from a marijuana smuggling business. Vilmos Zsigmond tells
of the crew being instructed to go to a hotel room where a woman
in a fur coat was passing out cash in lieu of paychecks. It wasn't all
so amusing. Sterling was later sentenced to forty years in prison for
drug smuggling. Two weeks before the movie's April 1979 release,
Goldberg was found handcuffed to a radiator in his Murray Hill
apartment, shot to death. And in the final perfect life-imitates-art
touch, Richard Condon himself weighed in with an article in the
May 1983 *Harper's* claiming that the release was deliberately sabo-
taged by the movie's distributor, Avco Embassy, so as not to embar-
rass Teddy Kennedy if he ran for the presidency in 1980.

For a film that delights in treating national tragedy and scandal with such flippancy, *Winter Kills* is remarkably free of malice or cynicism. It's the work of a filmmaker enjoying himself and the people on screen, his actors as well as their characters. After seeing the movie Richert had made of his novel, Condon told him, "The difference between us is that you like people and I don't."

Almost forty years later, *Winter Kills* has become a passage back to a time that seems very remote, politically and cinematically—a time when political scandals actually had to do with politics, and when mainstream movies had not succumbed to infantilization and spectacle.

Now, when the line between news and gossip and publicity has been erased—when the press and the public treat political sex scandals as if they had some political import—the illicit pleasure of *Winter Kills*, the feeling that we're peeking through a particularly ornate keyhole, reminds us that there was a time when we were sophisticated enough to actually believe Bill Clinton's admonition to Kenneth Starr that "even presidents have private lives."

Winter Kills also calls up the closing days of a decade that has proven to be the richest period in American moviemaking. There were still remarkable movies being made, and wonderful popular movies that were yet to come, like *E.T. the Extra-Terrestrial* and *The Empire Strikes Back*. But, more and more, daring and gutsy pictures went unseen. Two years later Jeff Bridges would star in another of them, Ivan Passer's *Cutter's Way*, and would see it, like *Winter Kills*, yanked from theaters after a week (in this case because United Artists was still reeling from the disaster of *Heaven's Gate*—which Bridges also appeared in—the previous month.)

Winter Kills comes down to that scene we opened on, Ralph Meeker and Eli Wallach in a cheap hotel in Tucson. In its odd way, it's the tenderest scene in the movie, although the associations it calls up need a bit of explaining.

The American filmmakers who emerged in the '70s were building on the genre films they grew up watching. John Ford is in the DNA of Sam Peckinpah's *Wild Bunch*, and Howard Hawks's *Scarface* is part of the heritage of Francis Ford Coppola's *Godfather*. It was, though, largely the big-name directors of the past—Ford, Hawks, Hitchcock, Capra, Wyler—who were familiar to movie audiences. No one except the auteurist critics were paying much attention to directors like Anthony Mann, Budd Boetticher, Sam Fuller, Nicholas Ray, and Robert Aldrich. That would have to wait for a new generation of critics, filmmakers, and programmers who would insist on the worth of the work those men did.

It's that tier of then-unacknowledged directors whom Meeker and Wallach call up, between themselves having worked with Mann, Aldrich, Fuller, John Sturges, Don Siegel, and Sergio Leone. The seediness of the setting suggests the low budgets these directors often had to make do with. And there seems something noble in the way the two of them are carrying on here: older, fatter, uglier, playing on some level a scenario they'd both played before, with precision and wit and the smoothness of old pros. And Richert suffuses the moment with admiration and affection, with the gratitude of a director who feels lucky to have the chance to work with them. These actors and the movies they represent are, Richert is saying, part of our shared popular culture. And he was saying it at a time when respect for the films they were associated with wasn't common.

Watching the scene now, you sense ghosts in the room beside Meeker and Wallach: the ghosts of an era that, like the heyday of the two aging mobsters they were playing, was fast drawing to a close. Going to the movies week after week in the '70s, you couldn't believe that there wouldn't be a time when its stream of amazing work—even if all that work wasn't good—would dry up. And there was no way Richert himself, coming along at the tail end of the era, could know that he would eventually be one of the ghosts populating the scene. To date, he has directed only three movies besides *Winter Kills*.

EYE OF THE BEHOLDERS:
EYES OF LAURA MARS

For Alyssa Reeder

BY THE TIME the Rolling Stones reach "Shattered," the last track of their 1978 album *Some Girls*, Mick Jagger has managed the equivalent of dancing his way through a horror movie. The setting is '70s New York—Fear City, as it was called in an infamous pamphlet produced by the police and firefighters' unions to scare the hell out of potential tourists. The images in "Shattered" are urban decay, straight out of a movie playing at a Forty-Second Street grindhouse, with rats and bedbugs and brains splattered over the streets. And instead of being repelled, Jagger sounds as if he's surveying a banquet before digging in. He sounds as if he wouldn't want to be anywhere else.

During the album's tour of New York City, Jagger muscles his way through "When the Whip Comes Down," a tale of a teen hustler funnier and gamier than anything John Rechy had come up with, and addresses the socialite status the Stones had achieved (the thing that made them a particular object of punk scorn) in the outrageously funny "Respectable," with its lines about the Stones consulting with the president about the problem of heroin. Even the Temptations' ineffable "(Just My) Imagination" gets the treatment, as if New York were no longer capable of containing the romantic dreams conjured by Eddie Kendricks's beautiful falsetto lead vocal on the original. In the Stones' version, the band's approximation of the original's dreamy tempo increases as the song fades, as if the pace of New York City will no longer sustain the conceit of a romantic fantasy even for the duration of a three-minute pop song. And Jagger, seizing the phrase "*running away with me,*" struggles to keep up with his band, as if he were trying to outrun reality and losing. This is the New York City of stratospheric crime rates and a blackout the previous year that had kicked off a looting spree. It was a time when the city almost went bankrupt and President Gerald Ford's response was summed up in the infamous *Daily News* headline, FORD TO CITY: DROP DEAD. It was the time of the city as pariah, fodder for the jokes of late-night TV comics and urban nightmares like *Death Wish* with Charles Bronson hunting muggers and other scum through the Manhattan night.

The insouciant, almost campy glee of *Some Girls* lies in its blithe determination to treat all this decay as a kick, an excuse for slumming good times. *Some Girls* wasn't made by people who were living or working on the margins. It doesn't have the raw-nerved jitteriness of the New York punk then being produced by artists as disparate as Television, Richard Hell, Suicide, or the reimagining of the city as the setting for glamorous, romantic fantasy being spun out by disco DJs like Larry Levan at the Paradise Garage and at more upscale venues. There are still people who feel that disco doesn't deserve mention in the same breath as punk—and some who still feel neither deserves mention in the same breath as music. But, like punk, disco was music made by people who lay outside of the power structures of record companies and radio stations dictating what got a publicity push, what made it on the air. The Stones' decision to lead off *Some Girls* with the disco-influenced "Miss You" was an honorable one, both the band's implicit rebuke to the vicious racism and homophobia of the anti-disco movement and their insistence that this reviled music was an honorable part of the R & B tradition they had always revered. *Some Girls* is music made by men who can sample the low-life and then return to their suite at the St. Regis. But it's well-heeled tourism that's as turned on by the grime as the glitter, and "Shattered" is the last bedraggled stop of a long night out.

"Shattered" moves with the sloppy propulsion of someone who's been through all New York City can throw at you. Jagger's vocal is a bruised shpritz, a prancing version of New Yorkers' time-honored practice of bitching about just how bad the city has gotten. The adrenaline-crash chorus behind him is sung in the cretinous voices of zombies rising from the Manhattan streets. And still at the end of the song Jagger is demanding more. Like many a transplant before him, he is still greedy for the city's energy, for its filth, for its scuzziness. And for Jagger being a New Yorker means boasting that you can take it.

The New York of *Some Girls* is the New York of *Eyes of Laura Mars*, released just two months after the album. This Manhattan thriller is a celebration of sleaze as high chic. It mixes the sleekness of limos pulling up to the curb for an opening-night party with the smell of the garbage awaiting pickup down at the corner. It's like a swank gathering where the stylish guests have to step delicately around the corpses lying on the sidewalk on their way into the mansion. Actually, in the gala art exhibition that opens the movie, the corpses are inside.

The pictures devised and shot by the wildly successful Laura Mars (Faye Dunaway), the fashion photographer being celebrated at that gala, are a singular blend of deadpan ghoulishness and bitch elegance. The designer duds her models wear play second fiddle to the scenarios she shoots: murders and car accidents in which the corpses, and the killers, are impeccably dressed—or undressed. Careful daubs of candy-red blood are applied to snowy, pleated tuxedo shirts. Immaculately made-up women in high heels and garters sprawl across luxe interiors, making death seem like the highest state of chic languor.

The images we see at Laura's opening night were in fact taken by the great photographer Helmut Newton, whose own blend of perverse eroticism and high-style sangfroid regularly sent people into a tizzy. Newton was often treated as if he were an arty pornographer or a cultivated monster of depravity, both of which descriptions probably delighted him. When Newton photographed the cool German beauty Nadja Auermann in a short dress and spiky leg braces, or placed an elegantly shod detached prosthetic leg next to the empty folds of her black evening gown, the gleeful naughty boy was lurking behind the provocateur's deliberation.

In the same year as *Eyes of Laura Mars*, Laura's photographic-double Helmut Newton published a book of photographs, *Sleepless Nights*, with an image that can stand for the movie's allure. *Security New York III* shows a man trying to force his way into the chained door of an apartment that a woman is trying to keep closed. It's one of those urban-horror-story scenarios especially common to New York City at this time. Except that this is Helmut Newton. The man—we see a sliver of his left profile and his left hand gripped on the doorknob—is wearing a blue suit, not the attire we expect of an intruder. The woman, her hair done up in one of those tight chignons that Newton favored, wears a lace-edged half-cup bra and a high-slit skirt. Her left arm is wedged against the door and her hands, the pointed nails immaculately painted in deep bloodred, grip the doorknob. It's unclear whether we are seeing a real threat or some kinky lover's game. Neither of them seems to be trying particularly hard to accomplish their task, and—as is often the case with Newton—you can't imagine much actually happening, for good or ill, if the man does manage to gain access.

In Newton's work, action is less important than the pose. Whatever is happening, the studied flippancy of the image comes from Newton's daring to see style and eroticism in a scenario that common sense would tell you is threatening.

That's what *Eyes of Laura Mars* does with a New York City that had accepted teetering on the abyss as the state of everyday life. The movie is shot in autumnal greys, a walk through the woods north of the city providing the only fall crimsons and golds. Except for a fashion shoot in Columbus Circle, we barely see direct sunlight. It's also a movie of night—a darkness that, at any given point, seems to show only what lies a few feet ahead. And yet, like few other movies, *Laura Mars* has the ability to make people look at its danger and sigh over a lost time they wish they could have lived in. You could say that's crazy, that that longing depends on ignoring just how bad the city was. The crazy triumph of *Eyes of Laura Mars* is that it paints the most dangerous scenario—a serial killer on the loose—and still revels in the place.

Dunaway's Laura Mars displays nothing of Newton's sense of humor. To the critics who accuse her of misogyny and crass sensationalism, she strikes the tone of serious artist, and the disjunction between the titillation of her images and the high-flown talk she uses about capturing the world around her to justify them is inherently funny, although there's no evidence it's a put-on. Given what is happening in her world, she may be right—especially when her associates start turning up dead, their eyes stabbed out with scissors.

Laura talks about "seeing" the images of murder and violence that populate her work as if they were psychic visions. The script, by John Carpenter and David Z. Goodman, hits on an irresistible gimmick to show just how attuned she is to those images. At the moment each murder is occurring, Laura sees the crimes through the killer's eyes. In effect, she becomes blind, her field of vision replaced by the killer's. This psychic kinship makes her a helpless witness to the grisly killings of her friends and associates. And since the audience can no more control the images that appear before us than Laura can, we're on her side. It's a great device, this psychic blindness always seeming to hit Laura at her most vulnerable moments, as she crosses a busy city street or when she's behind the wheel of a car. The movie is full of shots of the terrified, besieged Dunaway in some fabulous ensemble stricken immobile with fright as cars veer around her. This reaches a virtuosic climax when, at the end of the movie, the killer comes after Laura, and as she tries to get away, she can see only her own terrified retreating self.

The cornerstone of the movies' heritage of voyeurism is of course Alfred Hitchcock's *Rear Window*, in which James Stewart's war photographer, sidelined by a broken leg, is reduced to spying on his neighbors from the window of his Greenwich Village apartment. But Hitchcock had a strain of Catholic guilt running alongside his accomplished malevolence, his insistence that his movies were always just entertainments. When Stewart starts to believe that he has witnessed a neighbor's murder, Hitchcock plays on the audience's sense of complicity.

We've come wanting thrills, and Hitchcock is not about to let us shrink from the implication that the woman who's been murdered in the apartment across the way from Stewart has been murdered for our entertainment.

Laura Mars, superbly directed by the veteran filmmaker Irvin Kershner (*The Luck of Ginger Coffey, A Fine Madness, Loving*, the great Western *The Return of a Man Called Horse*, and the only good *Star Wars* movie, *The Empire Strikes Back*), isn't out to make us feel guilty. That the victims have their eyes stabbed out (barely glimpsed via the sleight of hand of Michael Kahn's editing) is less a metaphorical punishment for their collaboration in making murder look chic than the kind of clever jab at our own squeamishness that good thrillers trade in. Neither Kershner nor screenwriters Carpenter and Goodman are interested in making Laura culpable in the killings. They leave that to the killer, who offers it as a justification, saying Laura's photos stirred up memories of a deprived, sordid childhood spent with a streetwalker for a mother. It's the crazy person, the movie is saying, who blames his actions on the media (just as Ted Bundy, in the hours before his execution, blamed pornography for turning him into a serial killer), or the voices in his head, or the neighbor's dog. But *Laura Mars* doesn't deny the connection between artist and killer, either. They both have the same visions floating around in their heads, only the killer is crazy enough to act on them. The artist is only crazy enough to try and get them down on film, or the page.

It's a measure of the movie's sophistication that Kershner has no more trouble seeing Laura's photos as art than he has seeing crumbling and dangerous '70s New York as glamorous and exciting. It's a pity that, while the compositions are sometimes brilliant, the cinematography lacks the diamond-hard luster the milieu calls for. At least, the movie escapes the drab dishwater lighting that the director of photography Victor J. Kemper often brings to his work.

The movie is saying that danger is an essential part of glamour and of art. There's nothing particularly profound in this, and there may even be a trace of *épater le bourgeois* snobbery. But the movie is attuned to the sensual pleasures of movies, and of fashion. Kershner is saying that art and sex and urban life *should* get our blood racing. For the rest, there's Talbots and the 5:50 to New Canaan.

By the end of the '70s, there'd been a spate of movies in which the city was an inferno or urban madhouse, with one lurking danger after another—pictures like in *Taxi Driver, Dog Day Afternoon, Klute. Annie Hall* briefly revived the notion of New York as backdrop for romance, but when you get right down to it, a few pinkish sunsets that complement Woody's beige Ralph Lauren casuals does not a capital of enchantment make. The place in '70s cinema where New York *is* at its most enchanted is in the last forty minutes of John Guillermin's glorious, critically savaged 1976 remake of *King Kong*—for my money, the best of all three versions. In this *Kong*, the city has a soundstage storybook feel to it, a place where the miserably homesick Kong can make his way to the Twin Towers (gleaming against a Manhattan moon, they remind him of the mountains on his island), and a pair of would-be lovers can stop in their flight from him to pop into a deserted corner saloon and canoodle over a drink.

Laura Mars is perhaps the only New York movie from this era to groove on everything that looked so threatening in most of the other New York movies. Kershner finds the neurotic pleasure in the brittle, shallow milieu of late-'70s New York. He's alive to the way that the sophisticated and the grungy rub up against one another. Kershner gives us chic, minimalist apartments hiding behind scabbed foyers of pregentrification SoHo buildings; cavernous, seemingly abandoned warehouses housing a rich artist's studio; privileged lovers snuggling on fur blankets while, outside the window, the cruising ground of the docks offers far less cushy settings for more furtive couplings. Models in fur coats and expensive dresses can stage a mock catfight for the cameras in Columbus Circle while run-down luncheonettes and cobblers' shops are barnacled to the sidewalks across the way.

Like many of the best horror movies (*Jaws, Carrie*), *Eyes of Laura Mars* is at least partly a comedy, and its humor comes from the particularly New York intersection of high life and low life. That's the joke in a city where money and position can't insulate you from other people's hostility and resentment. When Laura, done up in cloak and riding cap, abandons a cab that's stuck in a traffic jam, tossing the driver a few bucks and getting out, he doesn't even pretend politeness. "Oh, like I got nothing better to do than sit here all day?" he asks. The characters floating around the edges of the movie are a collision of the glam and the quotidian. There are hangers-on, like the ex-husband (Raul Julia) who still has notions of using Laura as his meal ticket; handlers, like Laura's flamboyant manager, Donald (René Auberjonois, fuming his way through the movie like Franklin Pangborn after assertiveness training), who has to walk a line between coddling Laura and playing the stern task-master; glamorous models who drift through shoots and seemingly their own lives. The two most prominent are played by the model Lisa Taylor, with her grave bearing and hard, beautiful face, and the big-eyed charmer Darlanne Fluegel, who never had the acting career she deserved, getting to show off her comedy chops by playing the kind of winning ditz you might find in a '30s screwball comedy. There are also the less glamorous types who run the errands too minor for the talent to bother themselves with, like Laura's devoted driver, Tommy (Brad Dourif, with his explosion of Einstein hair and wild eyes), who did time for armed robbery but whose nervous hostility seems a perfectly normal response to the abrasiveness of the city around him.

Dourif, one of the finest American character actors for four decades now, gives the movie's best performance. Tommy is all anger and suspicion, yet he stirs up the audience's protective sympathy and trust. Nearly deranged and with both feet on the ground, Dourif's Tommy *is* New York City.

A bit higher up the scale of respectability is John Neville, played by Tommy Lee Jones, the detective assigned to investigate the murders, a working-class guy with aspirations to a better life who becomes Laura's lover. Neville has had some college, and while he doesn't approve of the chic emptiness around him, he doesn't treat it as the province of rich sickos. He leaves that to the other detective on the case (Frank Adonis), a quintessential New York Guido in a big-lapelled leather coat and smoked glasses. Neville can talk to Laura far more easily than the other cops, but he's still not of her world. And the romance that springs up between Laura and Neville is also part of the movie's humor and its logic, one of the cross-wired connections always possible in a city where the elite are bumping up against everybody else.

And at the center of it is Dunaway. Long before she played Joan Crawford—a fearless, terrifying performance that, were there any justice in the movies, would never have been treated as a camp joke— Faye Dunaway was a '40s movie star. She has the taut, neurotic emotionality of middle-period Crawford, the Crawford of *Mildred Pierce* and *Flamingo Road*, the one whose steeliness held together the quivering nerves of someone always on the verge of going to pieces. As Dunaway plays Laura, she's a woman who should never go anywhere without her business manager and a fainting couch.

Everything about her is tremulous and regal. Her haute-bohemian jitters fit right in with the general skittishness of the movie's atmosphere. And since the audience is as much in Laura's skin as she is in the killer's, Dunaway passes on the jitters to those watching. She's abetted by Theoni V. Aldredge's costumes, brilliant expressions of the way Laura is forever on the verge of losing her buttoned-up containment. She wears high-necked blouses with unexpected openings to reveal a flash of skin, long skirts with double slits. When Dunaway is concentrating on a shoot in the midst of Columbus Circle, her fabulous gams, shod in high-heeled suede boots, flash out of those slits so that she seems unconsciously exposed, and that sense of vulnerability is why we warm to Laura and why the possibility of violence here feels so physically threatening. Dunaway's performance in *Eyes of Laura Mars* is an essay in high-strung neuroses as high style.

By now the movie's embrace of sleazy urban chic has come to seem like something more, something like a gutsy and quixotic early salvo in the civil war that was waiting down the road. Two years after *Eyes of Laura Mars* was released, Ronald Reagan was elected president on a platform that located the very idea of America in the doggerel iconography of fantasies of small-town virtue. The city, especially New York City, was the repository of everything bad: welfare queens, liberals, and the gay men who Reagan's nonexistent AIDS policies would leave to die before any money was spent on research for a cure. A 1977 ABC News report on the rioting that followed that year's blackout quotes a New York City cop on the difference between working in this blackout and in the East Coast blackout of 1965. "In 1965 you were dealing with human beings," the cop said. "Now we're dealing with animals." If New Yorkers felt that way, imagine how much the rest of America hated the place.

Laura Mars sees the city teeming with gruffness and dirt even in ordinary times, its culture always in danger of being defined by its most shallow inhabitants. And in response the movie offers up something like civic pride masked as high sophistication. A friend from Tennessee once told me how, around the same time as *Laura Mars* came out, some relatives of his who were touring New York got into a cab and asked to be taken to an address on "the Avenue of the Americas." The cabbie turned around and said, "Say Sixth Avenue. Don't be a farmer." A true New Yorker, he preferred that corn be shucked elsewhere.

EVEN THE LOSERS: *BRING ME THE HEAD OF ALFREDO GARCIA*

Finally in a bower under the diaphragm
they found a nest of young rats.
One little thing lay dead.
The others were living off kidneys and liver
drinking the cold blood and had
had themselves a beautiful youth.

—GOTTFRIED BENN, "BEAUTIFUL YOUTH"

All I can say is that it was a very personal film, and I've no excuse for it.

—SAM PECKINPAH

THE TITLE HAS long been a joke, a ready-made punch line awaiting a name inserted at the end. *Bring Me the Head of . . .* your boss, your ex, the politician you most despise. When Sam Peckinpah's *Bring Me the Head of Alfredo Garcia* came out in 1974, it was the movie that was a joke. Those who had long championed Peckinpah were just embarrassed. In *New York* magazine, Michael Sragow called the movie "a catastrophe so huge that those who once ranked Peckinpah with Hemingway may now invoke Mickey Spillane." Praising Peckinpah's *The Killer Elite* the following year, Pauline Kael wrote of *Alfredo Garcia*: "The director appeared to have run out of zest for filmmaking."

And those were Peckinpah's admirers. The critics who already had their knives out for Peckinpah saw the film as more evidence of the decline of a once-talented director into grue and grime and general misanthropy. Only Roger Ebert seemed to see that the rawness of this brutalist fable, the story of an American drifter attempting to claim the million-dollar bounty a powerful Mexican padrone has offered for the head of the man who impregnated his daughter, was not a defect but its beating heart. "The movie is some kind of bizarre masterpiece. It's probably not a movie that most people would like," he wrote before concluding, "*Bring Me the Head of Alfredo Garcia* is Sam Peckinpah making movies flat out, giving us a desperate character he clearly loves, and asking us to somehow see past the horror and the blood to the sad poem he's trying to write about the human condition."

As the movie opens, we are by a quiet river in Mexico. Swans glide by, the sun turns the water's surface into reflected diamonds, and a young pregnant woman in a simple white cotton dress sits on a bank, dangling her feet in the water and cradling her swollen stomach. Everything about the scene suggests we are in a previous century, the slow pace of life at this hacienda, the caballeros on horseback, the room where the young woman is summoned by her father (Emilio Fernández, who played the brutal general Mapache in *The Wild Bunch*), lined as it is with imposing oil portraits of ancestors. The room is populated by women cloaked in what appear to be widows' weeds and fawning clergy standing as the padrone reads from an ancient Bible. But in this room the serenity of the idyll will not hold. It's violated by the authority in those portraits looking down on the proceedings, and in the unforgiving way that Fernández's padrone pushes aside the Bible with the abrupt dismissiveness that tells you that here he is God. The padrone asks his daughter for the name of her unborn child's father. She stares at him, refusing to answer, her sweet young face set in the pout of a kid trying to be tough. He asks again, and when she again refuses, he sets his goons to work. They tear her dress so that her breasts are exposed and then, because she is still not shamed, bend back her arm until we hear it break and she blurts out Alfredo's name. It's a shocking scene, not just because the victim of the violence is so innocent, but because the violence is a deliberate attempt to violate her purity, a symbolic rape, and because the violence doesn't matter to the girl's father, to whom she is already sullied goods.

And Peckinpah follows it with another shock: a displacing cut to cars bursting from the hacienda's garages, planes carrying henchmen away. We have been in the twentieth century all along, and this jolt that tells us so is Peckinpah's way of saying that the rot of the modern was always present in what looked at first like the romantic past.

At least as far back as 1962's *Ride the High Country*, perhaps the last great traditional Western in American cinema, the one sacred thing in Peckinpah's work has been the idyllic disappearing past. In his films, the past is rapidly ceding ground to a modern world that pushes out men as disparate as Joel McCrea's righteous Stephen Judd in *High Country*, the outlaws of *The Wild Bunch*, the scruffy frontier entrepreneur played by Jason Robards in *The Ballad of Cable Hogue*, even the modern-day rodeo star played by Steve McQueen in *Junior Bonner*. Even *Pat Garrett and Billy the Kid* is less about Kris Kristofferson's psychopathic Billy than it is a series of elegies for the aging character actors who turn up in the film only to die. The director's cut even includes an appearance from Peckinpah himself as, significantly, a coffin maker who announces to James Coburn's Garrett, "I'm gonna take everything I own and put it in the ground and leave this goddamn land."

Bring Me the Head of Alfredo Garcia is the only possible film this book could end on. Partly because it's by far the greatest of the films I've tried to make a case for, and Peckinpah the greatest of the directors represented in these pages.

Partly.

All the films in this book share an air of disreputability. *Alfredo Garcia* is a supreme example of how disreputability can be raised to the level of ecstatic and heartrending art. I have tried to avoid using the word *art* about the movies in this book, not just because I didn't want to inflate my claims for them, but because the word is used far too often to shut down discussion rather than to open it up. If something has been acclaimed as art, it's not just beyond criticism but often seen as above the mere mortals for whom it's presumably been made. It's a sealed artifact that offers no way in. It is as much a lie to claim we can be moved only by what has been given the imprimatur of art as it would be to deny that there are, in these scruffy movies, the very things we expect from art: avenues into human emotion and psychology, or into the character and texture of the time the films were made, or avenues into the context of our own time.

Had *Alfredo Garcia* been made by some exploitation hack, it would not have aroused the disgust that it did. Today it's unimaginable for a major studio to release a movie where every nicety has been sweated off. And even in 1974 that wasn't what anyone expected from a name director, even one with the reputation for violence and mayhem that Sam Peckinpah had acquired.

If the problem facing Peckinpah then was that *Alfredo Garcia* allowed his detractors to treat him as the bloodthirsty hack they had always claimed him to be, the problem may now be the very people who celebrate the director. At nearly every revival-house showing of

The Wild Bunch, knowing cheers accompany the close-up of William Holden saying "If they move, kill 'em" and the accompanying freeze-frame title: "Directed by Sam Peckinpah." Those cheers affirm the image of "Bloody Sam," the nickname he hated—affirm the very terms in which the director has been cartooned and dismissed. His detractors couldn't grasp the poetry in Peckinpah's mayhem, could see the savagery but not the tenderness, let alone the ways in which they are often the same thing. If Peckinpah's adversaries couldn't see those things, the new Peckinpah champions don't care about them. A few years ago I went to a rare screening of *Bring Me the Head of Alfredo Garcia* at the Brooklyn Academy of Music. The audience greeted the most extreme moments of Peckinpah's most painful and personal film with whoops of laughter. This wasn't the kind of uncomfortable laughter you sometimes hear triggered as a defense mechanism. It was unbridled hilarity at the worst violence, derisive sniggering at the scenes where the characters are at their most emotionally vulnerable. Peckinpah's most vociferous critics had sometimes said his films were fit only for cretins. Here the cretins claimed the director as their own.

What links *Bring Me the Head of Alfredo Garcia* to the other films in this book, its disreputability, is what allowed critics to originally dismiss it, what allowed that audience in Brooklyn to treat it as moronic swill. The movie stints on none of the grime and sweat and stench of the scramble for the title character's head any more than John Huston stinted on the grime and sweat and stench of the scramble for gold in *The Treasure of the Sierra Madre*, a movie that's the spiritual forerunner to this one. (At one point, Gig Young's mob henchman even identifies himself as Fred C. Dobbs, Bogart's name in Huston's movie.) It's not enough for Warren Oates's expatriate drifter Bennie to drive around with Alfredo's head in a rough canvas sack in the passenger seat of his beat-up convertible. Peckinpah gives us the ensuing swarm of flies carrion invites. ("*Tienes muchas moscas*," says the young boy who wipes Bennie's windshield when he stops at a roadside cantina.) It's not enough for Bennie to literally dig himself out of a shallow grave where the corpse of his murdered girlfriend Elita (the stunning Isela Vega) has been tossed in beside him. We see him coming up with the dirt in his mouth and a great gasp of breath as he breaks the surface. That gasp, that desperate groping towards life, is the entire movie in one involuntary sound. This is a movie about people who, like the aging outlaws in Peckinpah's *The Wild Bunch*, are defeated before they begin. It would be easy to try and turn the fortunes of *Alfredo Garcia* into a story of the triumphant emergence of a masterpiece by mentioning that its reputation has begun—*begun*—to undergo a reversal. Even a hint of triumph, though, seems all wrong for a movie haunted by the line "Nobody loses all the time," a movie where the only triumph is the triumph of integrity, the kind that gets you killed.

The line is Bennie's, played by Oates as a stand-in for the director, wearing Peckinpah's mustache and trademark dark glasses. Bennie wanders around the worst shithole tourist traps of Mexico, eking out a buck from whatever deals he can scrounge and from the tips he gets pounding the piano in seedy cantinas while leading silly tourists in drunken choruses of "Guantanamera." He really believes that "nobody loses all the time," and as soon as he says it we know he's doomed. It's no surprise that, like the outlaws of *The Wild Bunch*, Bennie's escape amounts to a form of suicide in which he'll take as many sons of bitches with him as he can. And yet, having insisted on every iota of dirt and deceit he shows us, Peckinpah also insists that from the same squalor can emerge something close to nobility of spirit, and that beauty can emerge from the sordid. The world of the movie is Yeats's "foul rag and bone shop of the heart" but without the ladder that Yeats writes of, without the possibility of physical escape. And yet this is also a movie that cannot pull its gaze from the idyllic vistas of an older Mexico, from a woman singing for her lover by a campfire, a movie that can't let go of the beauty that exists side by side with the ugliness. It's the work of a man with a death wish who loves life too much.

When Peckinpah made *Alfredo Garcia*, he was forty-nine and had ten years left to live. He had reached a point that most film-makers don't reach until they are much older, the point where nothing matters to them as much as getting their own particular truth on film. That doesn't always make for good movies. But even in clumsy ones it can make for undeniable emotional urgency. Peckinpah shared with another great American director of Westerns, John Ford, a love of the past. Ford's final film, the autumnal and furious *7 Women* (1966), a melodrama about missionaries in 1930s China, is old-fashioned even in the context of a rapidly faltering studio system. On one level it's an epitome of just how cheap and calcified the American studio system had become, reducing the director who was the great film poet of the unspoiled American landscape to painted backdrops and sets that are transparently fake. But the artificiality, and the strange fragility it imparts to the film, work as a reminder that the era of filmmaking epitomized by Ford is at its end. *7 Women* contains that era like a cameo contains the profile of a beauty from another century, and yet the emotional content of the film, particularly the performances of Anne Bancroft, Eddie Albert, Margaret Leighton, Sue Lyon, and Mildred Dunnock—and Ford's investment in the material—feel no less vital. Ford's lack of embarrassment at the melodrama, the movie's complete absence of concern with the stylish and the contemporary, feels like an act of sunset defiance.

By 1974, Peckinpah wasn't eulogizing the movie past but raging at its present. In her piece on the *The Killer Elite* (1975), "Notes on the Nihilist Poetry of Sam Peckinpah" (her favorite of all her work), Pauline Kael, who'd had a combative friendship with Peckinpah, noted that at the time his body looked as if it were on the verge of giving out. She once told me about having breakfast with Peckinpah in some hotel lobby, surrounded by business types taking early-morning meetings. Peckinpah sneered at the suits around him having their first coffees while he downed screwdrivers and thumped his pacemaker. This is how Rudolph Wurlitzer, the screenwriter of *Pat Garrett and Billy the Kid*, describes the Peckinpah figure in his 1984 novel *Slow Fade*, partly inspired by his time on the film's Mexico set: "the collapse in [the] once taut face, how the entire head seemed to hang by an invisible hinge, as if even the weight of gravity was enough to make it sag forward." By the time Peckinpah made *Alfredo Garcia*, rage and booze had been eating away at him for years. The production of almost every film involved a fight with the studio bosses. The film before *Alfredo Garcia*, *Pat Garrett and Billy the Kid*, an MGM production, had seen the worst interference of his career.

In the 1993 documentary *Sam Peckinpah: Man of Iron*, James Coburn, the star of *Pat Garrett*, and the producer, Daniel Melnick, recount how much James Aubrey, then president of MGM, hated the movie. Aubrey took particular exception to the way Peckinpah translated the poetic touches of Wurlitzer's script into a sustained elegiac languor. In the film the threat of violence comes with a deep acceptance that sudden death is an inextricable part of life in this place and at this time. All this was lost on Aubrey, the man whose triumph in his previous job at CBS had been bringing the network *The Beverly Hillbillies*. Aubrey wound up chopping twenty minutes out of the film. One of the film's editors, Roger Spottiswoode, remembers, "Aubrey was ordering scenes cut out for no other reason except he knew Sam didn't want them cut." The result, predictably, was an incoherent mess. (Since restored, the film now exists in three versions, the best of which, the 1988 "Turner Preview" version prepared by the editor Paul Seydor, restores most of Peckinpah's cut footage, giving it the fine tuning he did not.)

Laymen, people who expect executives to operate according to the common sense of sound business practices, can never understand why the studio moneymen would want to destroy their own product in such a way. The answer is that in Hollywood, ego is a far more potent currency than money. The chance for James Aubrey to ensure *Pat Garrett*'s box-office failure enabled him to say he was right and this director with his high-flown ideas was wrong. Which, of course, made it easier to control the next person who wanted to go against Aubrey's tastes. Peckinpah had already lost the heart to go against him. In his book *Peckinpah: The Western Films—A Reconsideration*, Seydor revealed that, unusual for a man who relished a battle with people he held in contempt, Peckinpah, exhausted, simply walked away from the fight with James Aubrey over *Pat Garrett*, allowing the film to go out in the studio-mutilated version.

It's in that context of exhaustion, or rather in the director's attempt to rouse himself from exhaustion, that we have to understand *Bring Me the Head of Alfredo Garcia*. As with the narratives in *Pat Garrett*, and especially *The Killer Elite*, the narrative in *Alfredo Garcia* is elliptical, oblique. The cadences, at first, feel muffled, and the stresses we'd expect in an action picture seem almost tossed away. Peckinpah was both refusing to go the usual genre route and developing a command of technique comparable to the impacted shorthand some writers develop in their later work. He was also stoking his most fevered obsessions, nurturing the slights and grudges and hatreds gnawing at him. This was what marked Peckinpah as an artist. Kael had seen *The Killer Elite*'s fantasy of a disabled intelligence agent (James Caan) as both an undisguised metaphor for Peckinpah's attempts to rehabilitate himself in the eyes of the suits and as a parable against them. *Alfredo Garcia* is something else entirely, a vision of a man who can see rehabilitation only in self-annihilation, who has come to see professionalism as a way of playing the game of the moneymen he despises.

In his 1973 *Playboy* interview Peckinpah said of the execs who bedeviled him, "The saying is that they can kill you but not eat you. That's nonsense. I've had them eating on me while I was still walking around." In *Alfredo Garcia* the buzzards are so presentable, they could almost pass as respectable businessmen. Played by Robert Webber and Gig Young, they're a pair of outwardly amiable mob henchmen (and, it's implied, lovers) who conduct their business with an efficiency more blasé than ruthless. When a barfly comes on to Webber in the cantina where they first encounter Bennie, he elbows her into unconsciousness without even looking at her. Whatever soul this pair had they sold it long ago, a transaction that seems to amuse Young. Threatening in a way he isn't as the head of a CIA-like organization in Peckinpah's *The Killer Elite*, Young walks through the movie with the ghost of a grin playing on his lips, a willingness to treat anything human as a grim joke. The bullshit he's trading in, the errands he carries out for his bosses, the desperation he encounters in Bennie, is all part of the human scramble in which he lost any stake long ago. He flicks away slivers of conscience as easily as he picks the bits of shell off his hard-boiled egg.

Bennie, on the other hand, can't cross the room without something eating at him. And that desperation is what marks Bennie as so out of place when he goes to visit the hotel suite headquarters of the organization Webber and Young work for (the very names sound like a law firm). Everything about the place is muted and tasteful, characterless and completely disposable—the golds of the furniture and carpeting; the bored high-priced call girls who sit around flipping idly through magazines while waiting to be summoned; the big shots who sit crunching numbers while delegating the wet work. They are a new style of gangster. The joke, of course, is that they could just as easily be studio moneymen, and you have the feeling that Peckinpah has been in offices and hotel suites like this many times before, has breathed this sterile air. Bennie's unwillingness to be a loser one more time is exactly what makes him so dangerous to men who long ago put human emotion on the debit side of their balance sheet. Bennie, in his cheap white suit and clip-on tie, is out of his depth. Any revenge he takes on these men is one he'll pay for not because of the tentacles of power they wield but because, like the Blob, their mediocrity absorbs whatever it encounters.

Peckinpah could be flamboyant or delicate or fearsome or clumsy and crude. He could never be mediocre. He hadn't abandoned craft or lost his zest for filmmaking in *Alfredo Garcia*. That stunning opening, and later a roadside shootout that sustains itself through rising and falling waves of tension and sudden shifts into Peckinpah's signature use of slow motion, rendering the lethal action indelible, are as brilliantly executed as any sequences he ever directed.

Next to those moments, the film can seem meandering, even unshaped. It isn't; it's unrushed. For much of its midsection we watch Bennie's journey with his girlfriend, Elita, to find Alfredo's grave and later, accompanied by the head that he has acquired at the price of losing Elita, Bennie's solo journey to give the men holding the purse strings their literal pound of flesh. Bennie and Elita ride in his battered white convertible, or pause by the side of the road while she plays the guitar and sings and they pass a bottle of wine. They talk of how they'll marry and where they'll go when they have the money he tells her he's coming into.

Elita dreams of returning to a peaceful town in Mexico she and Bennie once visited, the memory of which has never left her. They sound as if the fantasists of Harry Hope's bar in *The Iceman Cometh* had been set down inside a Jim Thompson novel. Even those dreams can't stay tranquil. Elita is a prostitute, Alfredo the former lover she'd been with days before she and Bennie set out on their trek. Alfredo was killed in a car accident on his way back from his farewell to Elita. Bennie's jealousy fuels his willingness to desecrate Alfredo's corpse, a desecration that horrifies Elita when she finds out just what will be required to prove Alfredo is dead.

No writer has approached the movie with more of an open heart than the film essayist Kim Morgan, who, in her battered Valentine of a piece, "The Love Song of D. Samuel Peckinpah," went right to the mournful core of the film's bruised delirium by writing this of the its most notorious moment:

> Forget "We'll always have Paris." What gets me to the core is
> Bennie repeatedly shooting a dead man and exclaiming, "Why?
> Because it feels so goddamn good!" Yes it does. Over-the-moon

crazy love dripping crimson romantic damn good—which is how it should always be.

Except that when it is that way, it scares people off.

Peckinpah, sometimes because of his own posturing and public remarks (from the *Playboy* interview: "There's women and then there's pussy"), has been derided as a misogynist. Some of his work leaves it an uneasy unanswered question, like Susan George's rape in *Straw Dogs*, which begins as a genuine attempt to ascertain where sex shades into violence and winds up an ugly macho fantasy. Some, the loathsome scenes in *The Getaway* (Peckinpah's biggest hit and worst movie), with Sally Struthers as a cheating wife whose public infidelities taunt her husband into suicide, seem to settle the question, and not to the director's credit. At this point I could mention that Peckinpah's work also includes *Ride the High Country*, where the hero gets himself killed because of his determination to keep a young bride from being gang raped. Or *Cross of Iron*, where a soldier who forces a woman to perform fellatio on him gets his penis bitten off. But there's something insulting and reductive about turning an artist's output into a balance sheet of correct and incorrect attitudes. Most people harbor contradictory and not always attractive impulses, and we shouldn't have to insist that artists tidy up theirs before we can appreciate or even examine their work.

Alfredo Garcia is Peckinpah's reckoning with macho, an attempt to treat male violence as a fallback position, a comfort zone for men who aren't strong enough to endure the violence women have long had to. It's a movie that is deeply ambivalent about male power, aware of its pettiness, its destructiveness, its emotional reductiveness, but also a movie that cannot give up that power because it serves as a survival mechanism in what remains a fundamentally hostile world. And yet it's that power, the padrone's demand for the head of the man who has trespassed on his property by sleeping with his daughter, that sets all the film's bloodshed in motion. This reckoning is at the heart of a movie that, for Peckinpah, is a desperate love story in which Bennie, and through him his creator, attempts to rise above the self-loathing that the director sees as the inevitable result of the unbridgeable gulf between men and women.

Peckinpah explores that gulf in a long, troubling scene in the middle of the movie. Bennie and Elita have pulled off the road to camp for the night and are interrupted by two bikers (Kris Kristofferson and Donny Fritts). The tone quickly becomes threatening, with the Kristofferson character leading Elita off to rape her while Fritts holds a gun on Bennie. When Bennie makes a move, Elita chides him to stay put. "I've been here before," she says, "and you don't know the way."

Take a minute to savor that line. Imagine it being said in some long-forgotten Western by an aging gunfighter to the greenhorn who's become his sidekick. Now think of it in this context, where a woman is telling a man she has to be tougher than he can ever be because, unlike him, she lives in a world where she's not expected to fight back. That unfair truth comes across even stronger in what follows. Kristofferson tears off Elita's shirt and strips her to the waist. Elita isn't just unbowed and unashamed, echoing the way the young pregnant girl stands before the padrone in the opening scene, but bold enough to slap Kristofferson twice, hard, right across the face. He returns the slap, but when it does nothing to intimidate her, nothing to make her stand any less proudly before him, he wanders off as if the anger and lust has leaked out of him.

Sometimes a movie's coherence is less narrative than thematic. Individual scenes might feel implausible even as they fit into the picture's larger scheme. That may be the case with what comes after that attempted rape. Elita follows Kristofferson, finding him withdrawn and ashamed. Now, in command of the situation, she reaches out to him, touching his beard as if, only now, she can respond to him as a human being. Very tentatively, they begin to kiss. Suddenly, Bennie, who has overpowered the other biker holding him at gunpoint, emerges, causing Kristofferson to brandish his gun. Bennie first shoots Kristofferson dead and then does the same to his buddy, who has rushed onto the scene. Elita runs to Bennie, tearful and relieved.

This is not a male fantasy. (Kristofferson's would-be rapist is, in turn, loathsome, humiliated, and, finally, dead.) It's a male nightmare. Bennie can hardly be expected to sit by while he believes the woman he loves is being raped. The sting of the scene is that by the time he arrives Elita has defeated the threat of violence. Bennie's understandable urge to protect her reestablishes violence as the ground on which all matters will be decided. The sequence is supremely uncomfortable for both men and women. For women because it presents a profound fear that becomes a moment of (for many, I'm sure, unbelievable) empathy. And for men because it presents a scenario in which no male response, from the most well-intentioned to the most vile, is adequate to the situation. When it comes to women, men, in Elita's words, "don't know the way."

Alfredo Garcia, opening in what appears to be Peckinpah's beloved past, gives us a world dirtied from the beginning, ruled by an archaic version of the male power from which all the violence in the film springs. Emilio Fernández's padrone may not have taken on the trappings of the modern world, but like the gutless corporate thugs who work for him he is just as happy to farm out his dirty work. The rub of it is that revenge is already beyond him when he gives his order, as Alfredo has been killed. And when Bennie appears before this ancient, foully corrupt old power broker in the movie's climax, the padrone treats the head as no more than a whim that has been fulfilled. "Throw it to the pigs," he orders after paying Bennie off. But Bennie, who has lost Elita and who has seen the trail of dead caused in fulfillment of this man's gruesome fancy, isn't going to be satisfied with money. He doesn't want answers as much as the thing he knows he will never get from this rotten, power-swollen old bastard: an acknowledgment of responsibility for the consequences he has set in motion. Fittingly, given the role of women in this film, it's the daughter, now a young mother, who decides the price her father must pay. "Kill him," she tells Bennie, the indignant hatred in her voice the thing that signals she is still morally alive. And Bennie, like some mangy knight doing a noblewoman's bidding, and seeing the chance to bring the blood and dirt he has had to wallow in inside this protected fortress, blasts the old man, and the guards surrounding him, out of this life.

It's a temporary victory, of course. Bennie can escape this room, the den from which the padrone rules his empire, but he can't escape the old man's revenge. The last shot of the film, an almost abstract close-up of the stuttering barrel of a gun firing at Bennie—we never see who's firing it, just the gun itself, the sound dying away and the smoke dissipating in the air—is an image of the death that awaits us all. But the wages of sin have already been paid. As Bennie leaves the room where he has killed the padrone and his thugs, he has to remember to go back for the

money. What he hasn't forgotten to take with him is the head
of Alfredo, his now-constant companion, his rotting Yorick,
who, like him, loved the same woman and has been defiled by
the same impersonal corruption. "Let's go," said William Holden
in *The Wild Bunch* before leading his band of outlaws to their
death. "Let's go, Al," says Bennie before making his own suicidal
gesture.

There was more good work to come from Peckinpah, but
Bring Me the Head of Alfredo Garcia is the last great film he made.
Peckinpah said it was the only film released exactly as he
wanted. Despite the slowly reversing critical evaluation, it remains
a masterpiece waiting to be acknowledged as such. Perhaps it's
not just the despair of the film, the dirt that seems to line every
crevice of every face, every auto, every piece of clothing that
has kept it from being acclaimed. The film, like the man who
made it, was, on some essential level, deeply out of sync with the
era in which he found his few years of acclaim. *Alfredo Garcia* is
not a young man's film. The young mavericks of American movies
in the '70s may have been working in classic forms, but they were
working with a sense of youthful excitement and discovery.
Peckinpah began his film career looking back longingly at the past,
and by the time he made this film he was already looking to his
own end. *Alfredo Garcia* is a death poem, a cry of anguish at the
beauty of the world, a mournful acknowledgment that his own
masculine nature would always keep him distant from the love of a
woman. It attempts to find articulation in a cry of pain, dignity in
the squalor that reduces humans to an animal level. If the movie is
the love song that Kim Morgan called it, it's the type of love that
the German coroner-poet Gottfried Benn identified in his poem
"Threat":

Know this:
I live beast days. I am a water hour.
At night my eyelids droop like forest and sky.
My love knows few words: I like it in your blood.

WHEN THE LIGHTS GO UP

"**HERE WE ARE** in a room full of strangers," the Bee-Gees sang in their song "Nights on Broadway." And now, much of the time, there's no one else in the room at all. The strangers we bonded with in dark movie houses, or the ones who made us feel cut off because we didn't share their pleasure or their derision, aren't there as we sit in front of our computer screens or our TVs. By the end of the '70s, audiences for movies like the ones in this book were already dwindling.

After *Citizens Band*, it was essentially over.

The fate of Jonathan Demme's comedy can stand as a tombstone for the era celebrated in the previous chapters. Paramount, which had no faith in the movie, dumped *Citizens Band* into second-run houses and drive-ins on May 25, 1977, the same day Twentieth Century-Fox began a cautious limited release of their new picture *Star Wars*. A week later *Citizens Band* was gone (it was rereleased in the fall with the terrible punning title *Handle with Care* and shown at the New York Film Festival, with no better results) and *Star Wars*, a movie happy to reproduce the stiffest and hoariest genre conventions, was on its way to the success that would open the door to the state of arrested adolescence in which American movies now reside.

The Force didn't manage to obliterate all genre movies from American cinema. There were still action movies and thrillers and even the occasional Western. And the new comic book and fantasy movies were not all pitched to the adolescent mind. Irvin Kershner went from *Eyes of Laura Mars* to the sci-fi noir of *The Empire Strikes Back*. Steven Spielberg, whose feature debut, *The Sugarland Express*, was one of the best genre movies of the '70s, contributed two of the cinema's great fantasy films, *Close Encounters of the Third Kind* and *E.T. the Extra-Terrestrial*. Richard Lester, after years in the commercial wilderness, brought his dry wit, and surprising surges of emotion, to *Superman II*. And the British director Mike Hodges, a master of the perverse, turned *Flash Gordon* into a great campy glitterfest of a space opera, the type of comic-book fantasy Fellini might have made had he been able to get outside of his own head.

But studios looking for the next blockbuster, and aware that the audience for that blockbuster would probably be adolescent, found it easy to shift away from the grit that had characterized '70s genre films. Now even movies ostensibly aimed at adults felt as if they had been made for people tired of the realities of the adult world, especially after Ronald Reagan's 1980 election, when the rah-rah and white-picket-fence clichés that had been laughed off the screen in the '60s started making a comeback. The '80s brought back the selfless mother who stays in a loveless marriage for the sake of the children and dies a martyr's death (*Terms of Endearment*); the undisciplined rebel who requires the military to make a man out of him (*An Officer and a Gentleman*); even, finally, those '60s troublemakers themselves, feeling guilty about all the ruckus they caused and embracing baseball as the thing that could make America great again (*Field of Dreams*).

Watching those movies with audiences who were eating them up was a little like seeing the Nichols and May routine where an overbearing mother manages to reduce her son the rocket scientist to a gibbering infant. Except that when you knew a lot of the people doing the gibbering, you didn't feel much like laughing.

Fittingly, it took a genre movie to allow the era's cozy hearth-
and-home mentality to eat itself alive. In Joseph Ruben's terrifying
1987 thriller *The Stepfather*, from a stinging script by the crime
novelist Donald E. Westlake, the main character is a serial killer
(Terry O'Quinn) who dreams of finding a family as perfect as the
ones he grew up watching on shows like *Father Knows Best* and
Leave It to Beaver. To that end he marries a widow with children
and sets about creating the flawlessly happy American family.
When, inevitably, real life proves not so perfect, this Robert Young
wannabe sets up a new identity in another town, murders his
existing family, and starts all over again. Watching O'Quinn mouth
every homily and cliché you'd hoped never to hear again inevitably
called up the folksy doddering image of Ronald Reagan. By the
time O'Quinn is hunting down the latest family to disappoint him,
the portrait of Reagan is complete.

This was still a version of Reagan the genial idiot, but it
reminded us that he was the genial idiot who supported the blood-
iest militaristic regimes in Central America and who, at home,
presided over the further impoverishment of the poor, oversaw the
beginning of the destruction of the middle class, and did nothing
while AIDS took a scythe through the gay community. O'Quinn
does his killing with a butcher's knife; Reagan did his with ballooning
military budgets and the dismantling of the social safety net. It took
a horror film to speak with the blunt language that political pundits,
not wishing to sound unreasonable, couldn't manage. "Ronnie is a
nice man," Clu Gulager had said of his costar in the final film
Reagan made, Don Siegel's *The Killers* (in which the future president
played a mob boss who slaps around his mistress, Angie Dickinson,
and in turn gets decked by John Cassavetes). How rude it would
have been to mention the blood dripping from his hands.

The phony cheer of the Reagan '80s has never fully vanished from the movies. And with movies shielding adults from complicated emotions, it became much easier to turn them to an adolescent and preadolescent mind-set. In American movies, things that might be expected to attract an adult audience are now almost entirely confined to the fall and winter awards season. And since most of those movies turn only the kind of modest profit Hollywood is no longer interested in making, the impulse behind greenlighting them seems to be as a way for the industry to convince itself it's still interested in what it refers to as "quality" films.

Occasionally, in the midst of the sequels and 3-D family animations and superhero blockbusters, a picture sneaks into theaters—never for long—and functions in something like the stealth manner of those deceptively happy endings that Hollywood directors used to fool the studio chiefs.

Released in August 2005, two weeks before Hurricane Katrina exposed the ugly new reality of American citizens as refugees in their own country, Iain Softley's supernatural New Orleans thriller *The Skeleton Key*—as good a ghost story as anyone had made since Robert Wise's 1963 film *The Haunting*—unwittingly dramatized the oppositions of rich and poor, black and white, tradition and progress, that Katrina brought into such stark relief. Andrew Niccol's 2011 sci-fi drama *In Time*, in which time has replaced money as the most valuable commodity and most of the American population is given a life span of twenty-five years, while the rich live on and on, was right in sync with the Americans who were galvanized by the then-burgeoning Occupy movement. And Scott Stewart's genuinely upsetting 2013 thriller *Dark Skies* used an alien-visitation scenario to offer a portrait of Americans living in a familiar world turned suddenly unknowable and nonsensical, a potent metaphor for the way the canyon of economic inequality has made nonsense of the rules of getting ahead by hard work and thrift.

Each of these three movies came and went without a ripple, maybe to be discovered on DVD or cable, but of course, in those formats, without the possibility of shared discovery that has always been at the heart of moviegoing. Moviegoing is rarely as thrilling as when audiences feel they are collectively hearing truths no one has bothered to say publicly. As they are released now, rushed through theaters in a few weeks, tossed onto the DVD and Blu-ray market and onto streaming and cable, movies become just more of the media noise. We're aware of them but, like that blog a friend tells us we have to follow or that TV serial getting all the attention, they are something we probably won't get around to.

In his 1962 essay "White Elephant Art vs. Termite Art," Manny Farber wrote:

> Movies have always been suspiciously addicted to termite-art tendencies. Good work usually arises where the creators . . . seem to have no ambitions towards gilt culture but are involved in a kind of squandering-beaverish endeavor that isn't about anywhere or for anything. A peculiar fact about termite-tapeworm-fungus-moss art is that it goes always forward eating its own boundaries, and, likely as not, leaves nothing in its path other than the signs of eager, industrious, unkempt activity.

But where, you have to wonder, are the "walls of particularization" that Farber said were a necessary condition of termite art at a time when the conditions of *how* movies are seen are so amorphous.

When digital culture has erased the boundaries determining not just when we see movies—during their initial release or months later?—but where we see movies—in a theater, on a flat-screen TV, on a laptop, on a phone?—and how we see movies—all at once or in pieces, an hour between dinner and bedtime or for a few minutes on the train home?—the medium itself is in danger of no longer being a communal experience and thus losing the aesthetic and social impact that that shared experience always held out as a potential. Now even the hits don't tell us much about the audience beyond their having developed the habit of moviegoing. Go to the opening weekend of almost any blockbuster and no matter how long the line was to get in, no matter how noisily they reacted, on the way out of the theater the audience seems to have forgotten what they just saw as quickly as Margaret Dumont forgets one of Groucho's insults. And their minds may already be turned to the next instantly forgettable blockbuster that will open the following weekend. This is consumption, not engagement. Contemporary audiences seem very far from understanding movies as either shared experience or private obsession. It's easy to pinpoint that absence of understanding in the ones who watch on their computers or phones. But the reduction of American commercial movies to product and spectacle have cut off contemporary audiences from the experience of sitting in a room full of strangers and feeling that the sheer size of the image was a connection to something bigger than yourself, something bigger than all of us.

ACKNOWLEDGMENTS

My agent, David McCormick, worked to get this book published when I was sure that the fat lady had sung. At Bloomsbury, Anton Mueller believed in it.

At the Vermont College of Fine Arts: Larry Sutin and Sue William Silverman saw early sections of the book. Their encouragement and editorial acumen made me believe I could finish it. As did Barbara Hurd, who showed me great kindness. By asking the right question at the right time, Robert Vivian confirmed that I had taken the right path. The camaraderie of my classmates made that path a pleasure to travel.

At the *Yale Review*: I am grateful to J. D. McClatchy and Susan Bianconi for giving me a place.

At the *Los Angeles Review of Books*: Merve Emre made a home for several essays in this book.

My students at NYU, Columbia, and the New School, many now friends, have given me some of the most rewarding work, and some of the sweetest moments, of my life.

To my brothers and sister, Steve Sarles, Dana Elder, Allison Elder, I love you always.

Love to my aunts, uncles, cousins, nieces, and nephews. I would like to single out my aunt Ellen Mercer, a rock in all kinds of heavy weather; my godparents, Vera and Morley Hodder; and my cousin Judy Sharos, the truest reader I know.

For friendship, support, love, advice, inspiration, etc., etc., etc.:

Corinna Andiel, Ace Atkins, Stephanie Barton, Jami Bernard, Ken Bleeth, the boys at the J. C. Rew Potent Potables Haberdashery, Britt Boughner, Fiona Breslin, Jan Budek, Buni, Ivanna Cullinan, Suzy Cullinan, Danielle Docheff, Katie Donaghy, Fred Elder, Champian Fulton, Frankie & Gracie, Dwight Garner, Robert Getchell, Ben Hett, Hilma, Jason, Franklin Jones, Kent Jones, John Kaye, Rachel Knopfler, Hillary Kelleher, Ed Kuhrt, Cree LeFavour, Maria McKee, Leandra Medine, Joyce Millman, Brian Morton, Dyan Neary, Silvano Nova, Lilly O'Donnell, Mutsumi Okoshi, Raquel R., Kalen Ratzlaff, Alyssa Reeder, Anna Rekosz, Garry Rindfuss, Carly Roye, Val and Bill Sarles, Craig Seligman, Gene Seymour, Martha Southgate, Willard Spiegelman, Barbara Sutton, Jim Verniere, Eileen Whitfield, Tracy Proctor Williamson, Lynn Zekanis.

Greil Marcus was my idea of what a critic should be well before he was my friend. That he continues to be both makes me very lucky.

Kaci Carolan has provided more support, more love, more faith, than anyone could reasonably expect. That, for her, is simply what it means to be a friend. To her friends, it's what makes her extraordinary.

Steve Vineberg and I have been having a conversation about movies and so much else for more than thirty years now. I couldn't love him any more.

Kim Morgan is a great friend, a master phone conversationalist, the Pai Mei of the claw machine. And her writing reminds me that cherishing your obsessions may be the most direct route to achieving the kind of the lyricism she gets down on page after page, and why reading her feels so goddamn good.

My life would be poorer without Laura Warrell and I cherish her.

Christina Paul has been every bit the tough-minded adviser I asked her to be when we met, and she has provided strength and sense as well as more laughs than is probably good for either of us. Thanks, Doc.

Chris Haydon has been a friend to my family during good times, an eloquent counsel during bad, and pretty much the definition of compassion. I am most grateful for him.

I thank Myrtle Zacharek for years of love and for bringing a twenty-four-toed blessing into my life.

To absent friends:

My aunt Florence Evans, who always treated me more like a son than a nephew, and who I still pick up the phone to call before realizing I can't.

My teacher John Knowlton, who carried himself elegantly, expressed himself with wicked wit, and was one of the first people to make me feel that I could be a writer.

Dan Ireland, a wonderful filmmaker, an eagle-eyed judge of acting talent, and just about the sweetest man I have ever met. This one's for you, Mary.

Pauline Kael, who first made me want to be a critic, who would have disagreed with much in this book, and who, having read it, would have picked up the phone and, in that breathy, lilting voice, said to me, "Oh, sweetie. You're nuts," which would have told me we were still friends. As if I ever had reason to doubt.

My mother, Eva, who never cared for movies but who loved reading and passed that on to me. She made me feel I was always loved and that she was always proud of me, even when I fell short of deserving that pride. I miss her every day.

Mom always said my dad looked handsome in his uniform as the head usher of the Central Square Theater in Cambridge,

Massachusetts. Apart from his time at that job, most of the movies he's seen in his life have probably been with me, beginning with dollar night at the movie house in our suburban town. I was becoming a serious moviegoer in the period covered by this book, and Dad took me to the pictures I wanted to see, whether the silly-ass MPAA ratings system thought I should see them or not. It's thanks to him I got to see the great films of the '70s as they came out. Even more than that, I'm grateful to him for a lifetime of work to make my life and my mother's life better, for his continuing and unceasing love, pride, and support, and his example of what it means to be a good and generous man.

The years I've spent with Stephanie Zacharek could be the work of someone who has pioneered a new genre—the melancholy screwball comedy—and I wouldn't have traded a goddamn one of them. I feel lucky I can say that my best friend, my shrewdest editor, and my perfect reader are all positively the same dame.

Charles Taylor
August 2016

FILMOGRAPHY

7 Women. Dir: John Ford. MGM, 1966.

Alice Doesn't Live Here Anymore. Dir: Martin Scorsese. Warner Bros., 1974.

Alice's Restaurant. Dir: Arthur Penn. United Artists, 1969.

All About Eve. Dir: Joseph L. Mankiewicz. Twentieth Century-Fox, 1950.

Aloha, Bobby and Rose. Dir: Floyd Mutrux. Columbia, 1975.

American Graffiti. Dir: George Lucas. Universal, 1973.

American Hot Wax. Dir: Floyd Mutrux. Paramount, 1978.

Annie Hall. Dir: Woody Allen. United Artists, 1977.

The Autobiography of Miss Jane Pittman. Dir: John Korty. CBS, 1974. TV Movie.

Baby Face. Dir: Alfred E. Green. Warner Bros., 1933.

Bad Day at Black Rock. Dir: John Sturges. MGM, 1955.

The Ballad of Cable Hogue. Dir: Sam Peckinpah. Warner Bros., 1970.

Beyond the Valley of the Dolls. Dir: Russ Meyer. Twentieth Century-Fox, 1969.

The Big Doll House. Dir: Jack Hill. New World Pictures, 1971.

The Big Heat. Dir: Fritz Lang. Columbia, 1953.

The Big Sleep. Dir: Howard Hawks. Warner Bros., 1946.

Black Emanuelle. Dir: Bitto Albertini (as Albert Thomas). Stirling Gold, 1975.

Black Mama White Mama. Dir: Eddie Romero. American International Pictures, 1973.

Black Sunday. Dir: Mario Bava. American International Pictures, 1960.

Bloody Mama. Dir: Roger Corman. American International Pictures. 1970.

Bob & Carol & Ted & Alice. Dir: Paul Mazursky. Columbia, 1969.

Bonnie and Clyde. Dir: Arthur Penn. Warner Bros., 1967.

Boss Nigger. Dir: Jack Arnold. Dimension, 1975.

Breathless. Dir: Jean-Luc Godard. Films Around the World, 1960.

Bring Me the Head of Alfredo Garcia. Dir: Sam Peckinpah. United Artists, 1974.

The Brown Bunny. Dir: Vincent Gallo. Wellspring Media, 2003.

Cabaret. Dir: Bob Fosse. Allied Artists, 1972.

Captain Nemo and the Underwater City. Dir: James Hill. MGM, 1969.

Carrie. Dir: Brian De Palma. United Artists, 1976.

China 9, Liberty 37. Dir: Monte Hellman. Allied Artists, 1978.

Chinatown. Dir: Roman Polanski. Paramount, 1974.

Cisco Pike. Bill Norton (as B. L. Norton). Columbia, 1972.

Citizens Band. Dir: Jonathan Demme. Paramount, 1977.

Coffy. Dir: Jack Hill. American International Pictures, 1973.

Convoy. Dir: Sam Peckinpah. United Artists, 1978.

Crazy Mama. Dir: Jonathan Demme. New World Pictures, 1975.

Cross of Iron. Dir: Sam Peckinpah. Embassy, 1977.

Cutter's Way (aka *Cutter and Bone*). Dir: Ivan Passer. United Artists Classics, 1981.

Dark Skies. Dir: Scott Stewart. Dimension, 2013.

Death Proof (released as part of *Grindhouse*). Dir: Quentin Tarantino. Dimension, 2007.

Death Wish. Dir: Michael Winner. Paramount, 1974.

Dillinger. Dir: John Milius. American International Pictures, 1973.

The Dirty Dozen. Dir: Robert Aldrich. MGM, 1967.

Dirty Harry. Dir: Don Siegel. Warner Bros., 1971.

Dirty Mary Crazy Larry. Dir: John Hough. Twentieth Century-Fox, 1974.

Dog Day Afternoon. Dir: Sidney Lumet. Warner Bros., 1975.

Dusty and Sweets McGee. Dir: Floyd Mutrux. Warner Bros., 1971.

E.T. the Extra-Terrestrial. Dir: Steven Spielberg. Universal, 1982.

Easy Rider. Dir: Dennis Hopper. Columbia, 1969.

El Dorado. Dir: Howard Hawks. Paramount, 1966.

The Empire Strikes Back. Dir: Irvin Kershner. Twentieth Century-Fox, 1980.

Executive Action. Dir: David Miller. National General Pictures, 1973.

The Exiles. Dir: Kent Mackenzie. Milestone, 1961.

Eyes of Laura Mars. Dir: Irvin Kershner. Columbia, 1978.

The Fast and the Furious. Dir: Rob Cohen. Universal, 2001.

Field of Dreams. Dir: Phil Alden Robinson. Universal, 1989.

Fighting Mad. Dir: Jonathan Demme. Twentieth Century-Fox, 1976.

A Fine Madness. Dir: Irvin Kershner. Warner Bros., 1966.

Firepower. Dir: Michael Winner. Associated Film Distribution, 1979.

Flamingo Road. Dir: Michael Curtiz. Warner Bros., 1949.

Flash Gordon. Dir: Mike Hodges. Universal, 1980.

Fort Apache, The Bronx. Dir: Daniel Petrie. Twentieth Century-Fox, 1980.

Foxy Brown. Dir: Jack Hill. American International Pictures, 1974.

The French Connection. Dir: William Friedkin. Twentieth Century-Fox, 1971.

'Gator Bait. Dirs: Beverly and Fred Sebastian. Dimension, 1974.

The Getaway. Dir: Sam Peckinpah. National General Pictures, 1972.

The Godfather. Dir: Francis Ford Coppola. Paramount, 1972.

Gone in 60 Seconds. Dir: H. B. Halicki. H. B. Halicki Mercantile Co., 1974.

Gone with the Wind. Dir: Victor Fleming. MGM, 1939.

The Great Escape. Dir: John Sturges. United Artists, 1963.

The Grissom Gang. Dir: Robert Aldrich. Cinerama Releasing Corp., 1971.

Gun Crazy. Dir: Joseph H. Lewis. United Artists, 1950.

Hail the Conquering Hero. Dir: Preston Sturges. Paramount, 1944.

Hard Times. Dir: Walter Hill. Columbia, 1975.

Hatari! Dir: Howard Hawks. Paramount, 1962.

The Haunting. Dir: Robert Wise. MGM, 1963.

He Walked by Night. Dirs: Alfred Werker and Anthony Mann (uncredited). Eagle-Lion Films, 1948.

Heart Like a Wheel. Dir: Jonathan Kaplan. Twentieth Century-Fox, 1983.

Heaven's Gate. Dir: Michael Cimino. United Artists, 1980.

The Help. Dir: Tate Taylor. DreamWorks, 2011.

Hickey & Boggs. Dir: Robert Culp. United Artists, 1972.

House of Wax. Dir: André de Toth. Warner Bros., 1953.

The Hurricane. Dir: Norman Jewison. Universal, 1999.

In Search of Noah's Ark. Dir: James L. Conway, 1976.

In the Heat of the Night. Dir: Norman Jewison. United Artists, 1967.

In Time. Dir: Andrew Niccol. Twentieth Century-Fox, 2011.

It Happened One Night. Dir: Frank Capra. Columbia, 1934.

Jackie Brown. Dir: Quentin Tarantino. Miramax, 1997.

Jackson County Jail. Dir: Michael Miller. New World Pictures, 1976.

Jaws. Dir: Steven Spielberg. Universal, 1975.

JFK. Oliver Stone. Warner Bros., 1991.

Junior Bonner. Dir: Sam Peckinpah. Cinerama Releasing Corporation, 1972.

The Killer Elite. Dir: Sam Peckinpah. United Artists, 1975.

The Killers. Dir: Don Siegel. Universal, 1964.

King Kong. Dir: John Guillermin. Paramount, 1976.

Kiss Me Deadly. Dir: Robert Aldrich. United Artists, 1955.

Klute. Dir: Alan J. Pakula. Warner Bros., 1971.

The Lady Eve. Dir: Preston Sturges. Paramount, 1941.

Lady Sings the Blues. Dir: Sidney J. Furie. Paramount, 1972.

The Last Detail. Dir: Hal Ashby. Columbia, 1973.

The Last Movie. Dir: Dennis Hopper. Universal, 1971.

The Last Picture Show. Dir: Peter Bogdanovich. Columbia, 1971.

The Late Show. Dir: Robert Benton. Warner Bros., 1977.

Le Samouraï. Dir: Jean-Pierre Melville. Artists International, 1967.

The Legend of Nigger Charley. Dir: Martin Goldman. Paramount, 1972.

Little Big Man. Dir: Arthur Penn. National General, 1970.

Little Caesar. Dir: Mervyn LeRoy. Warner Bros., 1931.

Lolita. Dir: Stanley Kubrick. MGM, 1962.

The Long Goodbye. Dir: Robert Altman. United Artists, 1973.

The Luck of Ginger Coffey. Dir: Irvin Kershner. Continental, 1964.

M*A*S*H. Dir. Robert Altman. Twentieth Century-Fox, 1970.

The Magnificent Seven. Dir: John Sturges. United Artists, 1960.

Malcolm X. Dir: Spike Lee. Warner Bros., 1992.

The Manchurian Candidate. Dir: John Frankenheimer. United Artists, 1962.

Mark of the Devil. Dirs: Michael Armstrong and Adrian Hoven (uncredited). Gloria Filmverleih AG, 1970.

Married to the Mob. Dir: Jonathan Demme. Orion, 1988.

McCabe & Mrs. Miller. Dir: Robert Altman. Warner Bros., 1971.

Melvin and Howard. Dir: Jonathan Demme. Universal, 1980.

Mildred Pierce. Dir: Michael Curtiz. Warner Bros., 1945.

The Miracle of Morgan's Creek. Dir: Preston Sturges. Paramount, 1944.

The Moonshine War. Dir: Richard Quine. MGM, 1970.

Mr. Majestyk. Dir: Richard Fleischer. United Artists, 1974.

Murder by Contract. Dir: Irving Lerner. Columbia, 1958.

Murder, He Says. Dir: George Marshall. Paramount, 1945.

My Darling Clementine. Dir: John Ford. Twentieth Century-Fox, 1946.

My Man Godfrey. Dir: Gregory La Cava. Universal, 1936.

Night Catches Us. Dir: Tanya Hamilton. Magnolia, 2010.

Night Nurse. Dir: William A. Wellman. Warner Bros., 1931.

Nothing Sacred. Dir: William A. Wellman. Selznick International, 1937.

Obvious Child. Dir: Gillian Robespierre. A24, 2014.

An Officer and a Gentleman. Dir: Taylor Hackford. Paramount, 1982.

Once Upon a Time in the West. Dir: Sergio Leone. Paramount, 1969.

Only Angels Have Wings. Dir: Howard Hawks. Columbia, 1939.

Outlaw Blues. Dir: Richard T. Heffron. Warner Bros., 1977.

Over the Edge. Dir: Jonathan Kaplan. Orion, 1979.

The Palm Beach Story. Dir: Preston Sturges. Paramount, 1942.

Paper Moon. Dir: Peter Bogdanovich. Paramount, 1973.

The Parallax View. Dir: Alan J. Pakula. Paramount, 1974.

Pat and Mike. Dir: George Cukor. MGM, 1952.

Pat Garrett and Billy the Kid. Dir: Sam Peckinpah. MGM, 1973.

Peformance. Dirs: Donald Cammell and Nicolas Roeg. Warner Bros., 1968, released 1970.

Pennies from Heaven. Dir: Herbert Ross. MGM, 1981.

Point Blank. Dir: John Boorman. MGM, 1967.

The Positively True Adventures of the Alleged Texas Cheerleader-Murdering Mom. Dir: Michael Ritchie. HBO, 1993. TV Movie.

Precious. Dir: Lee Daniels. A-Film, 2009.

Prime Cut. Dir: Michael Ritchie. National General, 1972.

Psycho. Dir: Alfred Hitchcock. Paramount, 1960.

The Public Enemy. Dir: William A. Wellman. Warner Bros., 1931.

Rafferty and the Gold Dust Twins. Dir: Dick Richards. Warner Bros., 1975.

Ray. Dir: Taylor Hackford. Universal, 2004.

Rear Window. Dir: Alfred Hitchcock. Universal, 1954.

Rebel Without a Cause. Dir: Nicholas Ray. Warner Bros., 1955.

Red River. Dir: Howard Hawks. United Artists, 1948.

The Return of a Man Called Horse. Dir: Irvin Kershner. United Artists, 1976.

Ride the High Country. Dir: Sam Peckinpah. MGM, 1962.

Rio Bravo. Dir: Howard Hawks. Warner Bros., 1959.

Road to Nowhere. Dir: Monte Hellman. Monterey Media, 2010.

Sam Peckinpah: Man of Iron. Dir: Paul Joyce. A&E Television Networks, 1993. TV Documentary.

Scarface. Dir: Howard Hawks. United Artists, 1932.

Shampoo. Dir: Hal Ashby. Columbia, 1975.

Silent Night, Deadly Night 3: Better Watch Out! Dir: Monte Hellman. International Video Entertainment, 1989. VHS.

The Skeleton Key. Dir: Iain Softley. Universal, 2005.

Smile. Dir: Michael Ritchie. United Artists, 1975.

Smokey and the Bandit. Dir: Hal Needham. Universal, 1977.

Soldier Blue. Dir: Ralph Nelson. Embassy, 1970.

Something Wild. Dir: Jonathan Demme. Orion, 1986.

Songwriter. Dir: Alan Rudolph. TriStar, 1984.

Sounder. Dir: Martin Ritt. Twentieth Century-Fox, 1972.

Stagecoach. Dir: John Ford. United Artists, 1939.

A Star Is Born. Dir: Frank Pierson. Warner Bros., 1976.

Star Wars. Dir: George Lucas. Twentieth Century-Fox, 1977.

The Stepfather. Dir: Joseph Ruben. New Century Vista, 1987.

Straw Dogs. Dir: Sam Peckinpah. Cinerama Releasing, 1971.

Sunset Boulevard. Dir: Billy Wilder. Paramount, 1950.

Super Fly. Dir: Gordon Parks Jr. Warner Bros., 1972.

Superman II. Dir: Richard Lester. Warner Bros., 1981.

Swing Shift. Dir: Jonathan Demme. Warner Bros., 1984. Mutilated studio release. Director's original cut on unreleased VHS tape.

Taxi Driver. Dir: Martin Scorsese. Columbia, 1976.

Tell Them Willie Boy Is Here. Dir: Abraham Polonsky. Universal, 1969.

Terms of Endearment. Dir: James L. Brooks. Paramount, 1983.

The Thing from Another World. Dir: Christian Nyby with Howard Hawks. RKO, 1951.

They Live by Night. Dir: Nicholas Ray. RKO, 1948.

Thief. Dir: Michael Mann. United Artists, 1981.

Thieves Like Us. Dir: Robert Altman. United Artists, 1974.

To Have and Have Not. Dir: Howard Hawks. Warner Bros., 1944.

The Town That Dreaded Sundown. Dir: Charles B. Pierce. American International Pictures, 1976.

Training Day. Dir: Antoine Fuqua. Warner Bros., 2001.

The Treasure of the Sierra Madre. Dir: John Huston. Warner Bros., 1948.

Truck Stop Women. Dir: Mark L. Lester. L-T Films, 1974.

Two-Lane Blacktop. Dir: Monte Hellman. Universal, 1971.

Ulzana's Raid. Dir: Robert Aldrich. Universal, 1972.

Vanishing Point. Dir: Richard C. Sarafian. Twentieth Century-Fox, 1971.

Vixen! Russ Meyer. Eve Productions, 1968.

The Warriors. Dir: Walter Hill. Paramount, 1979.

White Line Fever. Dir: Jonathan Kaplan. Columbia, 1975.

The Wild Bunch. Dir: Sam Peckinpah. Warner Bros., 1969.

The Wild One. Dir: László Benedek. Columbia, 1953.

William Shakespeare's Romeo + Juliet. Dir: Baz Luhrmann. Twentieth Century-Fox, 1996.

Winter Kills. Dir: William Richert. Embassy, 1979.

Women in Cages. Dir: Gerardo de León (as Gerry de León). New World, 1971.

You Only Live Twice. Dir: Lewis Gilbert. United Artists, 1967.

A NOTE ON THE AUTHOR

Charles Taylor has written on movies, books, popular culture, and politics for the *New York Times*, *Salon*, the *New Yorker*, the *Los Angeles Review of Books*, *Newsday*, *Dissent*, the *Nation*, the *New York Observer*, *Lapham's Quarterly*, and others. He is currently a regular contributor to the *Yale Review*. A member of the National Society of Film Critics, Taylor has contributed to several of the society's volumes, and his work appears in *Best Music Writing 2009*. He has taught journalism and literature courses at the New School, the Columbia School of Journalism, and New York University. Taylor lives in the New York area.